Choosing and Raising a Puppy...
HOW HARD COULD IT BE???

Trish Wamsat

Choosing and Raising a Puppy...
HOW HARD COULD IT BE???

 This book is not intended to replace appropriate diagnosis and/or treatment, when indicated, by a qualified veterinarian.

An Author's Dream Publishing, LLC

For Information:
An Author's Dream Publishing, LLC
P.O. Box 8217
Brownsville, Texas 78526-8217
www.anauthorsdream.com

ISBN: 0-9771091-6-X
ISBN: 978-0-9771091-6-6

Illustrations by Lissa Stiles
Photographs courtesy of DL Morgan, www.Morgankitson.com

Printed in the United States of America

ACKNOWLEDGEMENTS

This book would not have been written without the support and encouragement of the staff of Adobe Animal Hospital. Special thanks to Dave Roos, DVM, the creator and driving spirit behind this amazing place. Also to Suzie Bryce who came in like a hero on a white horse, to save us from ourselves! A huge thanks to all of the staff who generously donated their constructive criticisms and editing help. We have 20 full-time vets and more than 90 support staff at Adobe, and to get them all to agree on anything is nearly impossible. But they all agreed to help me with this; it was like having a built-in research department!

Another special thanks to Dr. Ian Dunbar, renowned veterinarian, author, trainer, behaviorist, and all around whiz kid who created Sirius Puppy Training 25 years ago and began the return to a friendship with our dogs. My writing here is heavily influenced by him and by Suzanne Clothier, who I think must be my long-lost twin (she got the brains AND the looks!). Suzanne is an internationally acclaimed dog trainer, speaker and author; her website, www.FlyingDogPress.com and her book, *Bones Would Rain From the Sky,* have helped many of my clients understand how important the RELATIONSHIP with their dog is.

D.L. Morgan at Morgan Kitson photography gave up an hour a week for six weeks to come and document the puppy class you will see in this book. She took AMAZING and relevant photos, and then was worried that they weren't what I needed; I'm sure you'll agree that they are PERFECT. Lissa Stiles drew the whimsical sketches; they were exactly the right touch.

Lastly, and mostly, thanks to my friends and family who have put up with my craziness for a very long time. Janet Kremzar, who gave me the little puppy that started me on my way back to loving the essence of a dog, not the obedience. My friend and mentor, Julie Bond, MS Animal Science, who took me under her wing and showed me that it was ok to open my mind and admit that there might be better ways. Janet and Julie have become my best friends and I am forever grateful to them for their wisdom and help. My family who have always rallied around me in tough times and accepted me for being me; my son, Ashton Van Tuyl; mom, Kay Blancet; sister and hero, Kathleen Wolski; and the late, great, Great-Grandma Hill who read me animal stories every night.

CONTENTS

FOREWORD

A number of years ago, a very joyful person came to work at Adobe. I was lucky enough to get this wonderful woman as my tech and as my friend. She taught me far more than I taught her. She taught me more about training and how to love dogs than I had ever known. She graduated from being my tech and took over Adobe Animal Hospital's training program. Our clients loved her. She taught with humor and love. She had her boundaries and taught those also.

Over the years that we worked together, we saw many sad sights. Dogs had to be put to sleep for fear aggression, separation anxiety, bad breeding, being vicious, and other reasons. Even sadder for me were the many times we saw animals who truly made their owners miserable and the owners would not put these animals to sleep out of guilt. We also saw many instances where people adopted rescue dogs that had severe problems and the rescue association had passed these troubles on to the new owner and put these people into bad situations. Many of these situations could have been avoided by a better selection process and by better early training,

The most important veterinary visit of a dog's life is at about 8 weeks of age. It is not important to protect the animal from disease but to start the training process of the OWNER. The pup's whole life is stretching out in front of us and if I can only convince the owner of a few important facts, I can make a true difference in the family's and the pup's lives. The facts are socialization, socialization, socialization.

Dogs need socialization and if they don't get it before 18 weeks of age, they may be scarred for their whole lives. Some dogs are naturally social but many are not. Families who don't socialize early enough may have shy dogs, fear aggressive dogs, bully dogs, or dogs who don't know how to interact with other dogs or with other people. And the sad part is that it is too late to learn. The dog with anxieties and fear doesn't know and can't learn a new way. Think how hard it is for us to change and we try to. Your dog is not motivated to make any changes.

I send the young 8-11 week old pup down to the local coffee shop on a Saturday morning. People and their dogs are there. I have the new pup meet everyone. Better yet, I have the new pet owner run, not walk to sign up for a puppy class. Puppy classes that make owners wait 'til the final vaccination lose the socialization time frame. These classes are afraid of infectious diseases but in all the years that Adobe Animal Hospital has had puppy classes, we have not had any cases of Distemper or Parvo that could be traced back to a class.

This book is about selecting your dog and then making that dog a truly additive feature in you and your family's life. I hope you enjoy the book as much as I have.

Dave Roos, DVM

PREFACE

I started training dogs professionally at 16 after a love affair with them that started about the time I was born. Saying I was a Lassie fan is like saying Dustin Hoffman's character in Rain Man was a Judge Wapner fan. I'm pretty sure my parents had moments where they imagined I was someone else's kid, out there in the yard pretending to be a dog, while the other kids were playing with trucks and dolls. In grade school, I had all kinds of crazy pets, including an invisible dog. I played horses instead of four square or hopscotch. I watched the Brady Bunch, hoping to get a glimpse of Tiger, the dog. I caught snakes and lizards and gave talks to classrooms full of younger kids about my pet cricket.

Thank goodness for high school, where I was actually able to OWN an animal! Future Farmers of America was my saving grace. My poor mom supported me through every minute of it. She even paid for me to take a professional dog trainer's course. It was a slick and impressive presentation. A LOT of money for a single mom with a crazy daughter and two younger, more normal kids at home, but she did it.

I jumped into dog training with all of the Lassie and Rin Tin Tin and Flipper images in my head. Then I started learning to train. With a choke chain and a sturdy leather leash, one that wouldn't break if you picked the dog up and hung it for a minute. It was sad but I was working with dogs; I bought into the violence and came to think of it as "tough love." The dogs were always happy to see me when I arrived at their homes, leash in hand. I never had treats with me, but they liked me anyway. It reinforced the party line of "food doesn't work in training" and that dogs worked to "please" people.

Some of the dogs bounced back well from the corrections, but some just folded.. The dogs walked as if on eggshells, pretty sure they could avoid being jerked, but not certain. They were careful not to act like dogs or have too much fun. Being "good" meant not getting excited when people came near, not exploring their world, actively ignoring other dogs they saw while out, and never moving from their "place" while in the house. It was incredibly impressive to the dog's owners and sadder and sadder for me. Everything that made a dog a dog was being suppressed. I used to wonder how Big Red and Lassie could have ever helped their families, had they been trained like this. But everywhere I looked, trainers were using the methods I had been taught.

I continued to train, but started working at "real" jobs as well. Soon I was a tech in a veterinary hospital. I taught training classes, was written up in newspapers and started to think I was pretty good. Life continued to steer me and I ended up at Adobe Animal Hospital in Los Altos, California. When I walked in the door, I knew I was home. I learned to *love* dogs again.

Adobe encouraged me to continue with my love of dogs. They nurtured my ongoing education. They allowed me to grieve over the loss of a patient I may have just met and rejoiced with me in welcoming the newest additions to a canine family. I have been blessed to know dogs and their families in the most stressful of moments. I have had the privilege of seeing true love. Adobe has always been on the cutting edge of the human/animal bond. To the management here, my becoming the staff trainer was a natural progression.

Adobe is where I learned that dogs CAN be trained without violence and pain. I adopted a beautiful puppy with special needs and realized that I didn't know how to train her without hurting her. WOW. That was powerful. So I went looking for methods that would work with my existing knowledge and make me a better and more effective trainer. One thing I find very interesting is that "in the olden days" trainers really didn't know much about puppies and normal puppy behavior. We didn't see them until they were six months old. Our training methods were too harsh for young puppies to tolerate! Now I spend an average of ten hours per week with 60 to 70 puppies. It's been so exciting to learn so much from them!

I continue to learn from my clients and their dogs, every day. I am so happy to be in a position to help them avoid the painful and scary training methods that are still so prevalent. I'm also very grateful to be in a position to redirect many relationships on the path to ruin and see the wonderful outcome of real understanding.

Try treating your pup as if he is Lassie. If you don't know Lassie, go rent some videos of the movies and the series. If we change our relationship with dogs from one of "commands" and "obedience" to one of leadership and trust, we will know the true joy of the human/canine bond.

Trish Wamsat

INTRODUCTION

Adobe Animal Hospital is one of the largest privately owned veterinary hospitals in the nation. It was established in the very early '60s by a young vet, fresh out of school, who provided care for animals of all shapes and sizes. Adobe has grown into a full-service, 24-hour hospital. There is a bedroom upstairs for the night doctors, for the rare occasions they can get a few winks between emergencies. The hospital has grown from a tiny, one-man practice to a bustling and efficient practice with more than 20 full time vets. We see EVERYTHING! From the calf requiring blood transfusions because of a dog attack, to the cat too late to save because of a raccoon attack, to the miracle of new babies, to the tragedy of an old friend who has reached the end.

At Adobe, we take care of the human/animal bond. There are few hospitals that have the dedication found here. To have an on-staff behavior counselor is an amazing benefit. This book includes tips and information from my 30 years of training and the expertise of more than 20 wonderful vets at Adobe Animal Hospital.

The thing I dread most in my working world is seeing the grief a family experiences when their dog has become aggressive. They are so blind-sided and wracked with guilt and confusion. How did it happen? When did it happen? How did I miss it? Can we fix it? Often, the answer to the last question is "should you try?" Some aggression can be minimized and trained and desensitized and managed. But what do you end up with and is it safe to do? Can you put in the constant, round-the-clock vigilance and can you and your family take the pressure and the liability? The answer is never to get there! Read on. Start the training now that will keep you from having to ask those questions.

Your puppy will be an important member of your family for a very long time. Some of the training seems time-consuming and you may think it's too much and you'll "get to it later." Very often, "later" is too late. There is nothing more important to your puppy's future than learning social skills and housetraining. These are the two things you cannot skimp on. Social skills includes being people-friendly, dog-friendly, not jumping on people, not trying to dash through doors, not pulling on the leash, and being comfortable around people in hats and people with walking difficulties. It includes being able to be around children safely and handling loud noises and chaotic moments. It includes being able to be safely restrained by strangers and not being aggressive around toys and food.

Social skills are easy to teach, as you'll learn in this book. It doesn't take long; most of it happens in the first few months and if you're not paying attention, those first few months are gone. We have a window of opportunity to socialize our dogs and that window closes at 18 weeks. Sure you can try to make up for it later, but nature is a pretty good teacher. Nature wants dogs to become cautious and distrustful as they become older

and more mobile. If they were in a wild environment, caution and fear would probably save their lives many times between 18 weeks and adulthood. But in our homes, caution and fear can easily become aggression.

Please make it your goal to introduce your puppy to ten strangers a day until he is 18 weeks old—an actual introduction, not just seeing them. If your puppy is fearful and not getting better, contact a trainer immediately! Meeting so many people during that time will go the farthest toward making your puppy a safe and sane member of your family.

PART 1
CHOOSING YOUR PUPPY

YOUR NEW PUPPY

You've been waiting forever! At least it feels that way. And now your new puppy is home. What on Earth comes next??

WELCOME HOME!

The following is a list of what you will need. You will find detailed explanations of why and how throughout the book.

- *A crate* - Honest. It really is important. Puppies need to be confined for their safety. A wire crate is best. Your puppy can see out easily, you can give treats through it easily, and wire crates are very versatile. Get the right size for your breed and if you're not sure, go to a full-service pet store and get help.
- *A bed* - for inside the crate. Go ahead and go as crazy as you want with this. Rarely, some pups will start shredding fabric, but most really enjoy a nice, soft bed.
- *Bowls* - use separate food and water bowls. They are more versatile and easier to keep clean. DO NOT get an elevated feeding platform.
- *Brush and comb* - buy a very soft brush for beginning grooming on a new puppy. Switch to more efficient ones as needed.
- *Collar and leash* - lightweight buckle collar and lightweight leash with an equally lightweight clasp.
- *Dog food* - puppy food is great for small breed puppies, but for puppies that will weigh more than 60 pounds at maturity we recommend a large breed puppy food or a good quality adult food. Whichever you choose, for a large breed puppy, the protein content should be 24% or less.
- *A measuring cup or measuring spoons* - SUPER important for measuring the right amount of food for your puppy.

- *Treats!* - a large assortment of pea-sized, soft treats for rewards. Freeze dried chicken liver is always a big hit.
- *Chewies* - rawhide, raw beef bones and even pig's ears for delicate chewers. No green toothbrush-shaped chewies. You'll need several of each type at the same time. This is not a place to skimp.
- *Squeaky and plush toys* - go as crazy as you'd like in this area, latex squeak toys are safer than vinyl. Make sure they're too big to be swallowed.
- *Lots of strangers* - to introduce your puppy to, every day until he's 18 weeks old. Then you can get away with just a few every day!
- *Interactive toys* - these include Kongs and other stuffable toys. Some dogs go for this and some don't. Don't spend a fortune without knowing your puppy will work to get food out. My favorite Kong treat is the Kong omelette! Kongs come with a recipe book that really helps.
- *An enzymatic cleaner* - for "mistakes" and messes.
- *Bedtime* - to know that a puppy's bedtime is 8:30 P.M.and no later than 9:00 P.M.

WHAT TO EXPECT AS YOUR PUPPY GROWS

The following explains what you should expect from your puppy/dog at various ages.

Younger than 7 weeks - Your puppy should still be with his mom. Mom teaches VERY important lessons in the 5-8 week old range and I don't recommend you bring home a puppy younger than 8 weeks old. Seven weeks is ok, but 8 weeks is best.

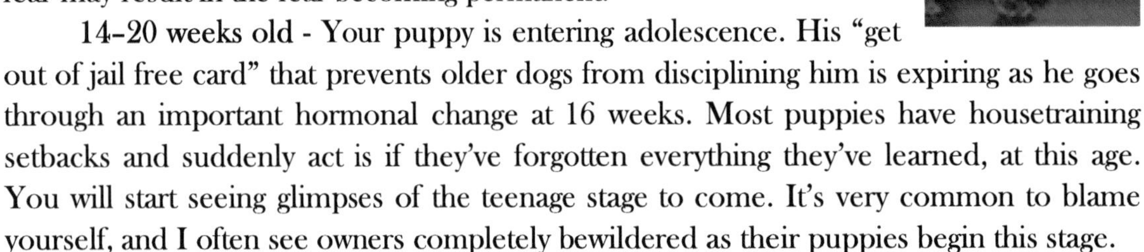

7-14 weeks old - Your puppy is very impressionable and sweet. He follows you around like, well, like a puppy dog! He may become frightened and it's important for you to "jolly" him out of that fear. That means don't act fearful, yourself, show him that there is nothing to be afraid of. Failure to jolly him or encouraging and validating his fear may result in the fear becoming permanent.

14–20 weeks old - Your puppy is entering adolescence. His "get out of jail free card" that prevents older dogs from disciplining him is expiring as he goes through an important hormonal change at 16 weeks. Most puppies have housetraining setbacks and suddenly act is if they've forgotten everything they've learned, at this age. You will start seeing glimpses of the teenage stage to come. It's very common to blame yourself, and I often see owners completely bewildered as their puppies begin this stage.

5-7 months - Your puppy is becoming more and more independent. He is starting to get into things that are easy to get into. A puppy who was formerly very happy to run, off leash, to the car with you, will suddenly decide to go for a run on his own. It is not safe to have puppies this age off leash as they are beginning to experiment with their independence and want to go and explore. They don't understand the dangers or that it's important to stick with you.

He is starting to surf your tables and countertops (if he can reach) and is probably barking at things he never even noticed before. Things like the garbage can in the street that you guys have walked past every day since he's lived with you or the fire hydrant across the street. Or the little old lady with the cane.

Puppies this age start another fear stage. We think they actually begin to see things that didn't mean anything to them before. It's a funny stage and very important. You need to perfect your jollying technique because this is going to last for a while. It's SO important not to let your puppy think he's protecting you or himself. It's SO important for you to make your puppy believe that you've got it handled and that he has nothing to be afraid of. Fears at this age can also become permanent and may become a phobia.

Confinement and supervision are also critical at this age. Prevent counter-surfing until he's over a year old and it's far less likely to become a habit. Prevent barking in the backyard and you won't have a "barky" adult dog. This is a critical age for preventing bad behavior from becoming bad habits.

7-10 months - Eight months seems to be the witching age! Even formerly perfect puppies seem to lose their minds at this age. If your male puppy is still intact, he may begin leaking urine when he sees another dog! It will just pour out of him. Neutering seems to fix this immediately.

Most puppies just start destroying things they've never paid attention to before. One puppy I know climbed a wall to get two framed pictures down so she could eat the frames. Previously a perfect puppy. My own puppy dragged a lawn chair 15 feet until it was under an awning protected from the rain. It seems that Simon didn't want to get wet while he pulled the stuffing out of it mouthful by mouthful. These incidents happened within days of these puppies turning eight months old and are only a TINY sampling of the stories I could tell.

At about nine months, the fear stage comes back with a vengeance. They often start barking at people and dogs and being weird and insecure. I have found that if not gently discouraged now, they will be fear aggressive at a year old. Many people think their dogs are protecting them at this age. This barking is not protective, it's fear-based and cannot be allowed. Jolly routine will get a workout again and may need to be accompanied by gentle but insistent scolding. It's very important that your puppy not associate being jerked on or hit or any other physical correction right now or he will forever blame strangers and may become aggressive or fearful around them.

I think that one of the biggest problems at this age is us! The humans. We see how much they've grown and changed, they're not tiny, helpless babies anymore and our brains tell us, "they should know better", or worse, "She knows it's wrong! She stops it when I come home/into the room..." fill in the blank. Dogs DO NOT want to make us mad. They only do what we train them to do. Puppies this age get more freedom and less supervision, when what they need is MORE supervision! Everything is new and exciting to them and they WILL explore it. What they do with it largely depends on where you are and what you do when they find it. Remember, IT'S NEVER THE DOG'S FAULT.

10-14 months - WHEW! Things start to calm down now. All but the tiniest of breeds will still be adolescent for another year, but it's much easier to handle. The hardest work is done! Now is the time to have some really good, safe fun with your dog. Enroll in fun classes and start competing in canine sports and games. Continue to prevent bad behavior and keep your dog busy! Any aggression should be dealt with immediately by contacting a great trainer who uses positive training methods like the ones you will find in this book.

15-24 months - Your puppy keeps getting better and better! Sweeter than ever and even starting to listen and being able to think again! Most dogs begin to become-who-they-will-be at this age. If you've seen any aggression, this is your very last chance to work with it before it becomes even more serious.

4-6 years - Your dog has been trained, you've settled into a good-old-dog routine and now your dog is becoming obnoxious. He may be barking at people on the street or becoming aggressive or destroying things or simply "not listening" to you anymore. This is a common disease called BOREDOM. Your dog was bred to do a job. You're probably taking him far fewer places and he's meeting far fewer people and he's bored out of his mind. So he starts inventing jobs...like replanting that tree in the yard or trying to scare the neighbor into the next county or chasing the mailman down the street from inside the house.

It's time to inject some meaning into your relationship! Get out there and get him into more classes! Teach him to pull a cart or carry a backpack. Take him out with you and buy him an ice cream. Shake up your relationship so it doesn't get shaken up for you.
10-13 years - it's probably time for another class or two. Get out and show off your beautiful senior dog. Active dogs stay active longer. Keep his brain in shape by entering him in local trick or costume contests. Have him certified as a therapy dog or teach him to swim.

The most important thing is that your dog was bred to perform a job. If you don't keep him working, he'll keep himself busy with or without you!

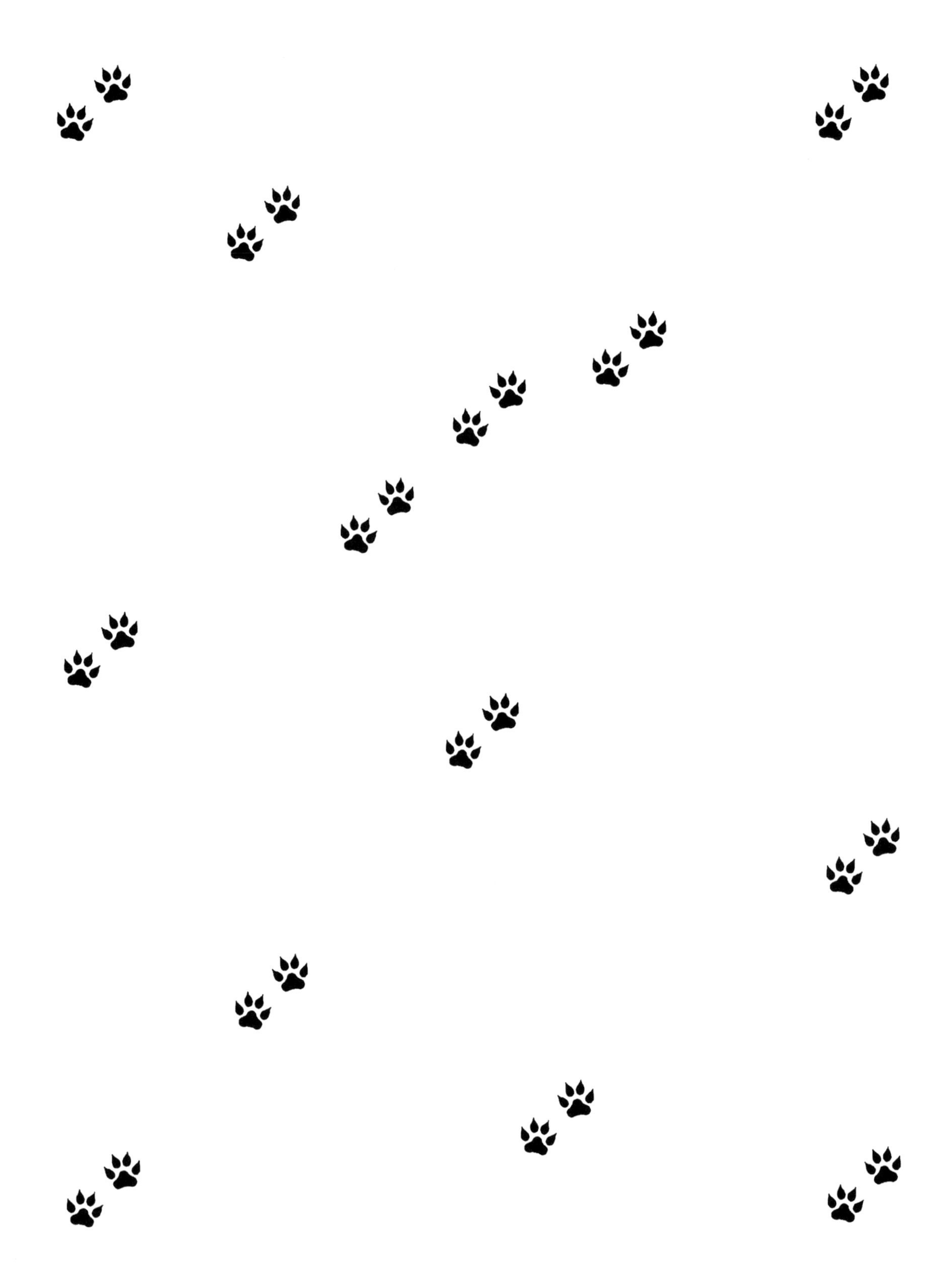

YOUR PUPPY'S BREED OR MIX AND WHY IT MATTERS

Breed does matter. Humans have been selectively breeding dogs for specific traits for thousands of years. Those traits appear to be "hard wired" into our dogs of today. The breed or mix of breeds you select (or that selects you) will have a huge effect on the dog you end up with. Genetics alone can dictate whether your dog marks territory or loves the dog park. His genetics will help decide if he is an escape artist or a homebody. Different breeds lean more toward certain characteristics so it's helpful to know what his genes are telling him.

Whether you have chosen a puppy already or not, you should read this chapter thoroughly. It will help you understand why your puppy does what he does and how what you can expect to change...or not!

PURPOSE

Breed traits don't have to be difficult to figure out. If you find out what a breed was originally bred to do it makes it pretty easy to figure out how they'll respond to training and life. In some cases it's important to know how long it's been since the breed was actually used for its original purpose and whether it has been bred for something different since then. For instance, the Mastiff was originally bred to go to war. Caesar wrote of them going into battle with him. Later they fought gladiators and even later they fought bulls and hunted poachers. They haven't had to do that for a while and have been bred to be more human friendly for hundreds of years. Now they're show dogs and companions. But some of the other very old breeds, for example the sight hounds, have continued to be bred for a specific purpose for thousands of years. Their purpose is very strong and dictates who they are. Sight hound refers to a type of dog that hunts by sight; that group of dogs includes some of the oldest breeds known to man. Even pet sight hounds with no training are very successful in "lure coursing" a contest that tests their ability to follow fast moving prey (a white plastic bag on a pulley system) through various turns and straight-aways.

On the other hand, while German Shepherds were bred to herd, they were also bred to guard. Most of their jobs in the recent past have been guarding jobs. They are bred to be suspicious and hard working and to do what it takes to protect their family and territory. Because of the work they have been bred to do, they adapt easily to a number of tasks and activities but they will always be on guard. They require a strong-willed and quick-minded owner to keep them from making the wrong decisions about who is a bad guy.

Fit

When selecting a breed, remember that breeders love their breed. That's why they have them. A Lab breeder will be fine dealing with the high energy level, exuberant greetings, holes in the yard, and mud on the rug. They love their dogs MORE because of these qualities and may not even consider that some folks might not appreciate those same qualities. Therefore, breeders may not mention that most Labs need really intensive training and supervision for the first two years of life, because it's such a part of living with the breed that they never give it a second thought! So don't be satisfied with talking just to breeders. Look for people walking their dogs and watch the interactions. Ask what it's like to live with the dog on a daily basis. Go to shelters or call and ask what the most common reason is that they see your breed in their shelter. Call local trainers and ask what the most common "problems" with the breed are. Most good trainers will tell you the problems are not problems with the dogs but with what the humans expect from the dogs, a mismatch of dog and owner. Most breeds are good for someone, but none of them are good for everybody.

THE TEST

Let's say you're looking for:

- a medium- to large-sized dog that will go running with you every day,
- it must be good with kids,
- enjoy camping and lakes,
- be a good house dog,
- a safe watchdog (alarm barking, not much in the way of biting),
- pretty healthy, not a lot of genetic problems,
- able to be trusted off leash with proper training,
- and may be a candidate for competing in a K9 sport if the kids decide they want to do that.

Now we'll take a look at the groups and what they were bred for. DISCLAIMER! The comments below are very generalized. They are based on my experience and the experiences of many other pet professionals. Of course there will be exceptions. I have seen vicious Golden Retrievers and a Labrador Retriever who won't fetch (retrieve). THESE ARE THE EXCEPTIONS.

BREEDS GROUPED BY ORIGINAL PURPOSE

The following is an easy way to group dogs to help figure out what they have been bred for and how that will affect them as pets:

- Hounds
- Working
- Herding
- Sporting
- Non-Sporting
- Toy
- Terriers
- Mixed Breeds

You can find the AKC's complete list at www.akc.org. If your dog is not an AKC recognized breed, just look at what the dog was bred for and use the following descriptions for guidance.

HOUNDS

The Hounds group includes both scent and sight hounds. Both types are driven to follow and catch. Some follow with their noses and some follow with their eyes. The one thing that holds true for all of them is that when they find something to follow, they GO. They will probably never be safe off leash in a casual environment. They have been bred not to be stopped by creeks or thorns or heat or desert sand. Most have been bred to fight to the death if they catch their prey. Their chase is often so focused that you can't draw their attention away.

Scent Hounds run with their noses on the ground. They will run into a street and under the wheels of a bus if the scent is fresh and exciting. This part of the group includes Beagles, Bassets, and Coonhounds. Keep in mind that these dogs are expected to "give tongue" (bark/bay/howl) while they are on the scent, so their owners can keep track of them. They are bred to have far-reaching, distinct voices. Your neighbors may not be thrilled. These breeds can be easy to train to a certain level if you motivate them properly. FOOD is a great motivator and I swear a Beagle will learn to drive a car for the right kind of dog cookie!

Sight Hounds run with their heads in the air, sometimes identifying their prey from a great distance. This part of the group includes Afghan Hounds, Borzoi, Greyhounds, and Whippets. Sight Hounds, because they are so visual, will often kill cats and other small animals that run through your yard. They are blazing fast and not many other animals can outrun them. Some may also be a risk to small children who are running. They tend to be nervous in new situations and love to sleep on the couch. Contrary to popular belief, they don't need a huge yard to run around in. Most of them do well with regularly stretching their legs at the dog park and on a walk with you. This group is where you will find some of the oldest breeds on the planet.

WORKING DOGS

Working dogs are dogs bred to work closely with people, not in a herding capacity. This group includes Malamutes, German Shepherd Dogs (who do herd, but have lately been used primarily for protection), Great Pyrenees, and Rottweilers (also formerly a herding breed). The dogs in this group are generally big, tough, and full of confidence. They have been bred for centuries to work for man under difficult circumstances. Many of the dogs were bred for "working ability," meaning not afraid of anything and completely reliable for their handler. Some breeds were bred to pull heavy loads over frozen ground and some were bred to keep bad guys away. These dogs are often hard to handle for the average dog owner. The sled pulling dogs are hard to control off leash and some should never be off leash without being in a fenced area. They were also bred for something I like to call "intelligent disobedience"; they will refuse to obey if the command doesn't fit what they think should be going on. Some of the protection breeds are just that. Protective. They need an experienced human, though, to explain what we need protecting from and what we don't. They often require a firm but gentle hand and will run roughshod over a quiet or non-assertive person.

This grouping also includes the livestock guardian breeds. While it might seem that they should be included with the herding breeds, they are really not bred to herd, more to be a part of the flock and fend off any kind of predator (furred, feathered, or human) that may pose a threat to their "family." These breeds are often NOT trustworthy off leash and will travel great distances to "patrol" their territory, regardless of whether or not it's really theirs!

The dogs that guard the stock include Great Pyrenees and the Kuvasz. They can be very protective with their family and can back up their bark with a ferocious bite if pressed. These can be good family dogs if you have great control over your kids' friends, otherwise the dog could get a little concerned. They will work for you; but remember, their natural work is lying in a field waiting to scare away coyotes and mountain lions. They're no slouches; they just act like it.

CANDIDATES

Of the working group, many of the breeds are very protective and may be fine with *your* children but keep in mind that children have friends and that friends will be around for the rest of your dog's life. Do you *want* a dog that has to be watched around children to keep him from getting overprotective? Early and enthusiastic socialization that continues through adolescence is critical. A reputable breeder who understands what you want in a dog is also a must have.

Some of the less enthusiastically protective breeds (provided they are not from a "working" background) are the Boxer, the Bernese Mountain Dog, the Portuguese Water Dog, and the Samoyed.

Boxers have energy until tomorrow and can be friendly and funny. Unfortunately, they are known for their predisposition for different kinds of cancer, and if not well bred, can be unpredictable.

Bernese Mountain Dogs are sweet, goofy, and not very protective. They wouldn't work as a runner as they are pretty heat intolerant and structurally often not very sound.

The Portuguese Water Dog is a good family dog but needs extensive socializing in puppy hood. This would be a good choice for our criteria. However, grooming needs are more extensive than most as they do need regular trimming.

Samoyeds can be wonderful family dogs but are not very trustworthy off leash. Their enormous coats require frequent brushing.

HERDING DOGS

Herding dogs are the dogs that actually move the livestock including Border Collies, Australian Cattle Dogs, and Corgis. These dogs move quickly and follow commands well, as long as you have taken the time to train them thoroughly. They have a tendency to think on their own and most of them really need to be in a home where they will have a series of very specific, demanding jobs. If you don't give them jobs to do, they will create them for themselves.

These breeds are very active and require a home where they will get lots of physical exercise, but more important is the mental exercise they need. Even catching a Frisbee for an hour a day is not enough mental stimulation for most Border Collies and they are commonly surrendered to shelters because they drive their humans and themselves mad. They are even known to self mutilate from boredom. I know of one Border Collie that actually lives and works on a ranch; she works full time moving sheep and cows and she still mutilates herself because it's not enough for her super brainpower. This brainpower is not a positive comment on the breed unless you are looking for a dog that will constantly challenge your training, decision-making and leadership skills. Dumb dogs are easy; Border Collies are NOT dumb.

Not surprisingly, dogs that are bred to herd cattle, such as Corgis, Australian Cattle Dogs, and Bouviers, are more aggressive and often nip to make their point. These dogs don't usually make a great choice as a companion for small children in the suburbs or city; they are very active. If you look on breed rescue sites for these dogs, you'll read the same stories over and over: "needs a large yard with room to roam," "needs to be the only dog," "no small animals," and "needs someone who will spend more time with him."

There are a few breeds that are somewhere in-between herding and guarding the flock. They were bred to move stock, but have had their drive to do it reduced through breeding for the show ring and pets. The Collie is one of these breeds. These dogs are active and versatile and usually very good with children when purchased from a responsible breeder. They are often very vocal, though, and the coat care is often too much for many people.

CANDIDATES

Of the Herding group, some are appropriate, provided they are well socialized, supervised, and trained. Some of the herding breeds have been used as protection dogs more than their original purpose in recent years and may be more than the average family bargains for. These breeds, such as the German Shepherd Dogs, the Belgian breeds (Malinois, Tervuren, and Shepherd), and Bouviers may be more inclined to be aggressive toward humans than may be fun to have as a pet, especially with children. Again, they will be fine with *your* children but may take their guarding duties too seriously with guests.

Many Shelties are too small to be a daily runner for much distance. They are often not good with children and may be fearful and shy, even of their owners. A Sheltie may be a good choice if purchased from an exceptional breeder at an early age and thoroughly and intensely socialized well through adolescence.

Collies would be a good choice, they have not really been bred for much beyond companions and show dogs for the past several decades. They are usually smart, empathetic, and easy to train. The smooth coated variety may be hard to get used to, as far as its looks, but it's a good, sound dog and fits all of our criteria. Health-wise, as always, buy from an experienced, responsible breeder. Collies are prone to eye and autoimmune problems and the breeder should have test results to show you when the puppy is as young as eight weeks old. Heat tolerance may be an issue for the rough coated dogs.

Australian Shepherds are sort of an all or nothing breed. Either they're wonderful or they're awful as a family pet. They can be aggressive and pushy with humans. As in all other cases, buying from a responsible and experienced breeder greatly reduces the risks. I would recommend an experienced person help you choose a puppy of this breed.

Bearded Collies are very bright, good with families (usually), and are not too terribly driven to work. Grooming in all of these dogs is limited to thorough, frequent brushing, although many people prefer to put Beardies in a "puppy cut" trim.

SPORTING DOGS

Sporting dogs are bred for hunting birds. Some are bred to flush them, some are bred to show the hunter where they are, and some bring them to the hunter after the birds been shot. All of them share a love for their work and a need for exercise. Some of these breeds make the transition from hunting dog to family dog easily and happily, others will go crazy in a non-working home. We've all seen the neighbor's Lab who just strolls around happily. But most of us know the dirty little secret of the Lab that doesn't "calm down" until he's 12. Cockers haven't really been bred to hunt as their main purpose in decades but remain in this group because...well, who knows? Cockers can make great pets or they can make your life miserable because of their health problems (mostly ears and skin) and terrifying propensity for biting.

This group is also divided into two groups, but not in the same way as the other groups. The others are divided by breed jobs; this group is really divided by show-bred or hunt-bred by breed. Dogs of the same breed, bred for different purposes will often look and act completely differently than their counterparts. The average family is most likely to be happiest with a show-bred dog from a very responsible, experienced breeder.

CANDIDATES

Many of the sporting breeds would be appropriate if they are from lines that will be happy being relatively inactive. The dogs that are bred to hunt want to hunt and they are often not good housedogs. Unless you hunt frequently or are an active dog-sport enthusiast you will not be providing enough exercise for most of these dogs. They are very purpose-bred and one would be wise to accept that about them.

Labrador Retrievers are big, strong dogs that have been bred to stand for hours in zero degree weather, then break through inches of ice to get what they want. They are bred to stubbornly search through brambles, briars, and barbed wire fences to find their master's duck. This translates to a dog that will hurt itself to get what it wants. Keep in mind that most Guide Dogs are bred from specific lines with specific traits and most *still* do not qualify. The very tasks that this dog is bred to perform requires independent thinking and a stubborn need to get its job done, no matter what. Many of these dogs require more exercise than even a very active owner can provide. Health testing by the breeder is mandatory. Labs are prone to Hip and Elbow Dysplasia, allergic skin, and ear diseases. Labs are also VERY prone to "dietary indiscretion"; a euphemistic term for "they eat everything and anything and often nearly die because of it." A well bred and raised Lab would be a great match for our criteria.

Golden Retrievers are similar to Labs in the tasks they perform but seem to have a "softer" personality. Many of them would be a great match to our criteria if they come from a responsible breeder. Goldens share many of the same health problems as Labs but, unfortunately, they also have a very high rate of devastating cancers. This is something that can't be tested for, so again, you must establish a great relationship with a wonderful breeder who cares deeply about the breed.

Brittanys and Springer Spaniels can be wonderful, happy housedogs as long as that's what they are bred for. If they are from hunting lines they will probably need more exercise and training than the average dog owner can provide. Springers seem to have a higher rate of reported aggression toward people than most other sporting breeds, a temperament malfunction. It is NOT normal behavior in this breed and needs immediate attention from a professional trainer or behaviorist.

Chesapeakes and Weimeraners are among the most "watchdoggie" of the sporting breeds and have the greatest propensity for human aggression among well bred dogs in this group.

NON-SPORTING DOGS

Non-sporting is a catchall group. It includes Chows, Schipperkes, Dalmatians, and Standard and Miniature Poodles among many others. The breeds in this group WILL require some research. For instance:

Chows, while they have lately been bred as pets, remain aloof, largely undemonstrative and don't usually do well with a home change as adults. Chows can be very aggressive with little or no warning. The warnings they do give are often imperceptible except to the most experienced "dog people."

Schipperkes are cute, quick little dogs that have HUGE teeth and, unless very well socialized at a very young age, will use them!

Dalmatians can be wonderful family pets in the right family. They are very active and protective and stubborn and often very sweet. The breed suffers from some severe health problems so make sure the breeder you are dealing with knows about and addresses them. Their health problems range from deafness to severe urinary problems and can be devastating for both dogs and owners.

CANDIDATES

Most of the non-sporting dogs won't work for our imaginary dog for reasons as varied as the group. But Dalmatians could be a match if they were from the right breeder. And Miniature and Standard Poodles are very athletic, often really good with kids, love to play, and would be a great match. An added benefit is that Poodles are light shedders and may be hypoallergenic.

TOY BREEDS

Toy breeds have been bred as companions for centuries. But remember, different people look for different things in a companion. Some people want a dog that will be an energetic but polite partner on a leisurely stroll; others want a dog that is happy with its feet never touching the ground! Some people want a dog that is everybody's friend and others want a dog to be theirs and theirs alone.

If you're looking for a friendly, outgoing, small companion for your kids, you should avoid Chihuahuas and Italian Greyhounds. Both dogs have a tendency to be jittery and both break very easily. They are very sensitive and tons of activity and noise usually don't make them very happy.

A better choice might be a Cavalier King Charles Spaniel or a Pug. I have met many Havanese that are happy and friendly but they (along with many of the toy breeds) can be hard to housebreak. This seems to be a genetics thing. Some lines do much better than others. Be sure to ask how long to expect to be housetraining your puppy. If the breeder says, "Oh, just use potty pads," RUN away. Someone who has adult dogs using potty pads in the house is not breeding for ease of housetraining. (Oh, the hate mail!)

TERRIERS

Terriers were designed to rid the world of vermin and to this day it is a purpose and they take very seriously! If you have a fondness for quiet, calm, and easy, this group is not for you. They are feisty, independent, and very, very busy. They don't do well in households with "pocket pets" as they are bred to hunt and kill small animals like that. On the other hand, if you want a dog who's ALWAYS looking for a game, digs moles gophers (and irrigation systems) out of your yard (or your sofa), and has a great sense of humor, this might be for you.

Terriers are "game" dogs that love people but will probably be animal aggressive and are usually not trustworthy off leash except in very controlled circumstances with lots of training. Most of them shed very little if they are properly groomed, which is probably the biggest reason they end up in homes that are not really prepared for them; lots of people buy dogs based on one appealing factor and the terriers low shed and often small size is their downfall. Those people often expect a "normal" dog! Some are less active than others but most of them need lots of activity in their lives.

CANDIDATES

Of the Terriers, Soft Coated Wheatens could work, as could Airdales from the right breeder and with proper training.

American Pit Bull Terriers, American Staffordshire Terriers, and other "Bully" breeds deserve a special mention. There are lots of reasons not to own one of these breeds not the least of which is the way the general public perceives them.

A well bred dog of this type can be a treasure to a family. They are bred to be friendly, goofy, trainable, and very forgiving of all human meanness. They were, literally, bred to have their person pull them out of the middle of a fight with another dog and show NO AGGRESSION toward the person. They were bred to let people do horrific things to them without ever showing resentment or fighting back. Dog fighting was outlawed in Louisiana less than three decades ago but it is still widely practiced there. We're not talking about a bunch of drug dealers getting together to see whose dog is toughest; we're talking about a highly organized, multi-million dollar industry, with magazines and books and how-to videos. In much of the south, it's considered an art, a beautiful thing (as barbaric and horrifying as you and I may see it). And the dogs are worth tens of thousands of dollars.

The fighting dogs of the south were (are) destroyed if they showed the slightest sign of human aggression. Human aggression is the one thing not tolerated. For decades they were bred not to signal that they were about to attack, not to stop attacking regardless of the submissive signals from their opponent, and to bite and hold as long as possible. But above all, they were bred NEVER to turn those weapons toward a human. Now the weaponry has escaped. It is loose in the form of poorly bred and understood dogs. And now the breed has to pay.

The problem with Pit Bull type dogs is that they are rarely well bred anymore and when they are poorly bred or mixed with other breeds they may lose the character that makes them so safe for humans to be around.

They must be considered NEVER safe around other dogs. They will probably appear to be safe until they are one to two-and-a-half years old. At that time, their instincts kick in and you will see the real dog. Lots of Pit Bull type dog owners get lulled into a false sense of security and think that because their dog was so well socialized as a puppy and young dog, he will be fine with other dogs as an adult. And some will. But the majority will surprise and horrify everyone that loves them by becoming a fighting dog. Serious and deadly. That is the reason that NO HUMAN AGGRESSION can be tolerated from this type of dog. They are NOT "just like other breeds," and it's not "all in the way you raise them." They are DIFFERENT. It's what makes them loveable and it's what makes them dangerous.

MIXED BREEDS

Mixed breeds can be the best or the worst of their heritage. Mixed breed dogs are often hardier and healthier than their purebred counterparts. It is true for most of the puppies, but some are destined to suffer getting the worst genes from each parent. The mixing of genes dictates that it's a toss up. The better the health and temperament of the parents, the better the health and temperament of the puppies.

The best thing about mixed breed dogs is that sometimes they do get all the best of both parents and many people feel a great sense of satisfaction bringing home an underdog. There are absolutely wonderful mixed breed dogs in homes and there are many more languishing in shelters.

The worst thing about mixed breed dogs is the irresponsibility that goes into creating them. It's not cute and it's not funny when an irresponsible dog owner "accidentally" has a litter of Chow/German Shepherd mixes, or a litter of Cocker Spaniel/Poodle mix. If the dogs are being "accidentally" bred (or purposely mixed), that is your first clue that the parents of the pups are not well bred. They are being bred through either neglect or greed and either way, your and the dog's best interests are not of primary interest. Mixed breed dogs can be wonderful and deserve loving and responsible homes, but it's "let the buyer beware" as far as temperament and soundness go. The puppies in shelters are proof that the "breeder" didn't even care enough to find homes for them.

The other bad thing about mixed breed dogs is that if it's a mix of very different breeds (German Shepherd and...say, a Golden Retriever) first, there are LOTS of bad genes floating around in there, looking for a matching one. Bad hips, bad skin, bad temperament, bad allergies. These are all deficits in the breeds and if they are reproduced, they will be horrible. Also, the proper temperament for both of these breeds is very different; some dogs can be neurotic because of conflicting responses to stimulus. Where a Golden is bred for friendliness with strangers, a German Shepherd is bred to be suspicious and aloof. Which one will the mixed breed obey when they meet a stranger on the street? It could be one or the other or it could be both leading to fear and aggression.

To a certain extent, it's all a crapshoot. You do the best you can with the information you have and hope for the best. But not to do the work is irresponsible and begging for trouble. The right puppy is a mixture of genetics, socialization, and hard work on the part of the breeder and you. It does pay off.

RESULTS OF OUR SEARCH

The most important thing to take with you from this short, very incomplete summary is that dogs are "hardwired" for certain traits and you should make sure they're traits you will LOVE. Every breed will have something you could like about it, but you should make sure you are really hearing and understanding what their shortcomings are, even when presented in a positive light. The dog we started out looking for in the beginning sounded pretty easy. By narrowing the field, we can eliminate everything from the hound group (not safe off leash), the toy group (too small), much of the working group (too big, can't run with you) most of the terrier group (not safe off leash especially camping). The candidates listed above are good choices for most families. I hope you take with you that a breed's physical appearance is truly only skin deep.

CHOOSING A BREEDER AND YOUR PUPPY

Choosing the right puppy will prove to be a critical part of your future. Puppies bred by responsible and caring breeders are worth the time and effort it takes to find them. MOST breeders, even those with the best intentions, don't do the best possible for their puppies, but this guide will help you separate the good from the bad. True, good puppies can come from bad breeders, but do you really need to take that chance?

The most important thing for you to know is that your puppy's life experiences before you take him home will contribute to his ease of training and ability to adjust to new experiences. Somc of what he will be like is predetermined by genetics, but many undesirable qualities can be recognized and helped by an alert and dedicated breeder. A good breeder will recognize a fearful or shy puppy and employ techniques to increase his confidence and give him tools to feel safe in his world. More importantly, a good breeder will recognize that a particular puppy is not the right one for an inexperienced dog owner (like you) and will keep you from accidentally making a tragic mistake.

The wrong puppy can be bad on so many levels. For example, seeing your new puppy being afraid of everything the world has to offer. Hearing that the barking and growling and biting he does actually IS aggression and that your daughter's friend's face will never look the same since that bite your puppy gave her. Being told by your veterinarian that your dog will need Prozac and training to be able to live with just a tolerable degree of anxiety. And watching the littermates you adopted turn into aggressive, fearful brats by the time they are a year old. Yes, there are lots of horror stories about bad matches and bad dogs and, yes, they are true and, more importantly, they are preventable. This guide will help you make the best choices when you are faced with picking the right puppy. And that starts with picking the right breeder.

Screening the Breeder

The following are suggestions for choosing a great breeder; the suggestions are meant for the average person who wants a super, smart, and friendly companion dog. Regardless of the breed or mix of breeds a good breeder will:

- Ask what you have to offer the puppy
- Ask who will be caring for the puppy
- Ask what your past has been with the dogs in your care
- Ask what your living situation is
- Ask what you expect to have your living situation become
- Ask if you are familiar with possibly negative traits of the breed
- Have had the litter examined by a veterinarian

He/she will also:

- Have started a deworming program with the puppies
- Have socialized them with all shapes and sizes and colors of people
- Have exposed them to household sounds and sights
- Have given them lots of different obstacles to explore
- Have left the puppies with their mother regardless of being weaned
- Have a guarantee of health and show an interest in helping you be successful with your pup

And a good breeder will expect you to ask questions too:

- How long have you been involved with this breed (or mix) of dogs?
- How often do you show/compete with this breed and have you won anything of note?
- How many dogs do you have?
- How many people have been to visit the puppies and at what age did the visits start?

- How many of the visitors have been children and of what ages?
- How do you handle the puppies?
- How do you prepare the puppies for their future homes?
- How do you prepare them for housebreaking? For crate training?
- What made you decide to do this particular breeding? What can you tell me about the father of the litter?
- What health tests have been performed on the parents? And the puppies?

The following are some important things to know about the answers.

BREEDER BACKGROUND

You are looking for a breeder who is aware of everything about their breed or mix. They know the good qualities and the potential for bad. They should warn you if Hip Dysplasia is common in their breed or if the dogs are prone to hearing or vision problems. Toy breeds, for example, are VERY prone to having Luxating Patellas (kneecaps that slip out of place). This can be a painful and expensive condition. The breeder should let you know the pup's knees have been checked and that they will give you the veterinarian's report in writing.

A breeder who doesn't show or compete or perform with their dog in some way probably shouldn't be breeding. Lots of people have pet dogs that they breed with no knowledge of the problems they might produce. The reason they bred the litter is often that they wanted a puppy from this dog or that she's really pretty. They have seldom done any research; including making sure their own dog is free of hip or eye problems before breeding. They also seem unaware that finding homes for puppies is easy; it's finding homes that won't give them up when the going gets tough that is the problem. Unless the other answers prove otherwise, this is a "backyard breeder." Please don't support their decision to add more dogs to the world by buying one of theirs.

The next group of questions addresses the handling, socializing and preparatory training of the pups. Make no mistake! Early handling and training is critical.

EARLY DEVELOPMENT/SOCIALIZATION

In a perfect world, you are looking for a breeder who knows that they are shaping babies' minds. The breeder would proudly explain that the puppies have been exposed to many different footing surfaces, that they have been held and petted by many different people of all shapes, sizes, and colors, and have played in lots of different kinds of boxes, tunnels, ramps, and even water in a little mock pool. The breeder would let you know that the puppies have been together and with their mom even though she weaned them weeks ago. Puppies learn so many important things from their dog families, things that will remain with them for the rest of their lives.

Many breeders, even very well thought of ones, still separate the puppies from their moms when they start eating real food. This results in pups that are bossy and pushy and lack self-control. They are not used to rules. Mom would normally let them know that she is the boss and they'd better obey the rules. Mom should be allowed to growl at them and even snap at them as needed to keep them in line. These lessons carry over to remind the pup that he is not the end-all-be-all.

The world isn't perfect, though, and a breeder who even comes close to being perfect is quite a find!

At the *minimum*, the puppies should have:

- Been handled by many visitors
- Stayed with mom 'til they're at least seven weeks old
- Been indoors and outdoors
- Come from a mom who is housebroken

A breeder who doesn't allow visitors until the puppies are eight weeks old is setting them up for fear and failure. A breeder who keeps the pups until they are 12 weeks old had better be taking them for rides in the car, walks on the street, and having over 50 people in to visit them (not all at once of course). They should be used to hearing the TV with loud shows and even war movies. They should be used to the dishwasher and fans and water hoses. The puppies should be sleeping in a crate, alone, and learning about being housebroken. Otherwise, I would avoid buying a pup from this breeder. There is work that goes along with keeping puppies 'til they're older and if the breeder doesn't do it the puppy suffers.

JUST SAY, "NO"

I have seen too many puppies purchased by well meaning owners because the puppy "lived on a farm" and the breeder was so nice. The problem with puppies being raised on a farm is that not many people drop by. Often the parents aren't really well socialized and the puppies are worse than the parents. Dogs raised in this manner are often fearful and shy. Their lives are miserable and so are their owner's lives. They often never learn to enjoy new things and may become aggressive.

Other reasons to walk away:

- If a puppy is reluctant to come to you, don't buy it.
- If a puppy is aggressive with you, don't buy it.
- If a puppy looks sick, don't buy it.
- If a puppy is so submissive it stays on its back, don't buy it.
- If a puppy is interested in the world around him, but not you, don't buy it.
- If a puppy briefly approaches you, then goes off to explore, don't buy it.
- If a puppy growls when you handle its feet, don't buy it.
- If a puppy growls or snaps when you take a crumpled paper towel away from it, don't buy it.
- If a puppy hides, grovels, and crawls toward you, don't buy it.
- If a puppy freezes when placed on the ground on a different surface than what it's used to, don't buy it.
- If a puppy barks in alarm when you approach, don't buy it.
- If the puppy was separated from its mother earlier than seven weeks, don't buy it.

THE IMPORTANCE OF MOTHER

If you are not allowed to meet the pup's mother, find another litter. If the mother is aggressive or very shy, her puppies will have a good chance of being aggressive and/or shy. The mother dog should act appropriately for a dog of her breed. In other words, if she's anything other than a guard dog (which you shouldn't even be looking at!), she should be happy to see you and happy to be petted and fussed over. Being "protective of her puppies" is not good and you will need to find another litter.

Aggression is a serious condition. It cannot be cured and often requires intensive management to keep people safe. People who end up with an aggressive dog have their work cut out for them and often end up having to euthanize their beloved family member. They also, often, end up living with the reminder that their beloved family member disfigured another beloved family member.

BUYING LITTERMATES

If a breeder is willing (or eager) to sell you two puppies from the same litter, find another breeder. A good breeder will know that it's not good for littermates to be raised together. It actually increases the work for the new owner and cuts down on the attention

each puppy receives. If puppies are not separated, they become two halves of one dog. They rely on each other for everything and often develop separation anxiety and aggression problems. They find it easier to communicate with each other than with humans so they turn to each other when humans confuse them. To raise littermates successfully they should be kept separately, walked and trained separately, crated separately, and they should receive all of their attention separately until they are about a year old. As you can see, rather than two puppies taking pressure off of the family, they are actually a lot more work. If you want two puppies, raise one first. Make sure he is socialized, housetrained, and trustworthy, then add a puppy to your household.

DON'T FORGET DAD!

It's common for the pup's father not to be on the premises. But you should ask what he's like and meet him if possible. Ask to see pictures of him and a pedigree if a purebred. If a breeder is selling purebred pups and can't show you pedigrees for both parents, find another litter. Breeders who are making wise decisions are using pedigrees to make them. Ask the breeder of the mixed breed pups why he chose that dog to father the litter and if you can meet him. The answer should make it clear that thought went into the selection and that the puppy's health and temperament were the priority.

PEDIGREES AND HOW TO READ THEM

Some breeders "line breed." They breed within the same lines to produce the best quality. You will see the same kennel name over and over. You may even see the same dogs listed multiple times. When done by experienced breeders this can eliminate problems in the "line" or family of dogs or it can bring certain qualities to the surface. Sometimes these are good qualities like coat texture or quality and sometimes they are bad qualities, like Hip Dysplasia or Epilepsy. Line breeding cannot create bad qualities; it can only expose qualities already there. Most breeders who line breed are extremely experienced and responsible and know what the pups will be like even before the breeding. On the other hand, some sellers have a brother and sister or a mother and son and breed them with no thought to what they could be producing. Those "breeders" are after the almighty dollar and you should run away!

A pedigree is a family tree. The pup's parents will be the first two dogs listed. If you are buying a purebred, it's important that at least one of these have Ch. before its name. Ch. is short for the title Champion. If the breeder is breeding for performance, the titles will follow the dog's name. Different sports have different titles and the breeder should be happy to point them out and explain their meaning. Farther back in the pedigree, at least 80% of the dogs should be titled in something.

BAD BLOOD

Some puppies are bred in puppy mills, a common term for a puppy farming operation where dogs are treated as livestock. The mother dogs often live their entire lives in rabbit-style hutches and small pens. Puppy mills were an accepted part of the dog world after the dust bowl and depression. Brokers went to bankrupt pig farmers and left them dogs of breeding age. The farmer just had to feed the dogs and raise the puppies to weaning age, and then the broker would come and get them, pay the farmer, and take them to a central warehouse where they were distributed to various pet stores and Sears. Yes, the puppies that used to be sold through the Sears catalogs were from puppy mills.

Today, puppy mills are pretty much the same except that they are older and the breeder dogs they use are the result of generations of breeding for only one quality: salability. The puppy mill brokers often send buyers on trips to unsuspecting and eager breeders where they replenish their stock with the occasional "champion bloodline" dog. They also go looking for highly desirable and rare breeds like Havanese and Cavalier King Charles Spaniels. Much of the reason breeders of excellent quality dogs can be hard to buy from is that they are very wary of their dogs ending up in a puppy mill. The puppy mill buyers are very smooth and smart. There are still brokers and warehouses and even auctions where breeding stock is sold

But now we know more than we did then. We know that dogs raised in that manner are not healthy physically or mentally. We know that dogs should not live as livestock and we know that breeding a dog every time it comes into season is bad for it. We know that breaking a mother dog's jaw to keep her from biting the person who is reaching into her cage to take her puppies is not acceptable. We know that raising puppies on wire with little food and no toys is wrong. It makes puppy mill puppies nearly impossible to housebreak and often they learn to eat their own stool because it's the only thing to play with in their cage. While I hate to say this, be extra careful if you're dealing with a breeder in Nebraska, Kansas, Oklahoma, Texas, Arkansas, Pennsylvania (the Amish are well known for having puppy farms), and Missouri. These states are home to MANY puppy mills and brokerages.

Websites are another way for puppy mills to sell their wares. Their websites don't say they are a puppy mill. In fact their websites are often very commercial and catchy. They will have pictures of a dog or two in their home; they will have lots of pictures from satisfied buyers. But they WON'T have pedigrees or win photos or pictures of their home-bred Champions. They WON'T have links to the breed clubs they are members of and they won't GRILL you before you buy a pup.

They will be VERY familiar with shipping protocols and they will dazzle you with their love of their dogs. Keep in mind that you are about to pay them MANY TIMES what the broker will for their puppy and they want you to BUY.

Puppy mills are insidious. I boycotted the American Kennel Club for years because I felt they needed to do something to stop puppy mills. They did, they instituted DNA testing for frequently used sires and dams. The testing would ruin puppy mills because their record keeping is abysmal and they wouldn't want to spend more money on their dogs. Puppy mill puppies are frequently not who their registration papers and pedigrees say they are. I have firsthand experience watching "papers" change a non-registered puppy into a registered one. If a puppy or dog died, the mill would keep the papers and use them for another dog down the line.

I was very happy to know the change that AKC made would make things better for dogs but the puppy mills, knowing they needed a kennel club affiliation, created their own kennel clubs. Pet stores and brokers all over the country will tell you that the new kennel clubs are better than the AKC. They are abusing dogs in mind numbing numbers.

REGISTRIES AND REGISTRATION

If a purebred puppy's registration is with the CKC, ask to see the registration. If it says anything other than Canadian Kennel Club, the puppy's parents or grandparents are from a puppy mill. Period. The people who bought the parents probably didn't realize that they were from a puppy mill and might not appreciate you telling them that they are. Just be glad you know and go find another litter. Some people think of buying puppy mill dogs as rescue and in a very real sense, it is. But every time they sell a puppy it's on the back of a broken, beaten, and lonely dog just trying to stay alive. Buying their puppies enables them to stay in business.

Acceptable all breed registries would be:

- American Kennel Club (AKC)
- United Kennel Club (UKC)
- Canadian Kennel Club (CKC)

Most other registries were created to get around the strict rules of the above. Many of the puppy mill registries make their initials sound like the acceptable ones to cash in on inexperienced puppy seekers.

"Papers" usually refers to the registration status of the puppy. Registration may be limited or full, depending on the breeder and the quality of the puppy you are purchasing. Never accept "I'm waiting for the papers" when it's the parent's papers you are discussing. It's possible that the puppies' papers may be delayed (very rarely) but the owner MUST have the parents registration certificates for you to look at and, as mentioned above, the pedigree.

PUTTING IT ALL TOGETHER

If you follow the advice given here, chances are still high that emotion will kick in and color your puppy search. It's often a good idea to enlist the help of a friend or relative you can share this information with but who is not emotionally invested in the puppy. Take him or her with you and make sure you take this chapter as well. If the breeder's story changes between you talking with him on the phone and when you get there, run away! Have your assistant keep track of stories and remind you if you start losing focus. Emotion is a beautiful thing and you will be able to use it all on your new puppy when you find the right one. Don't buy a puppy because you feel sorry for it.

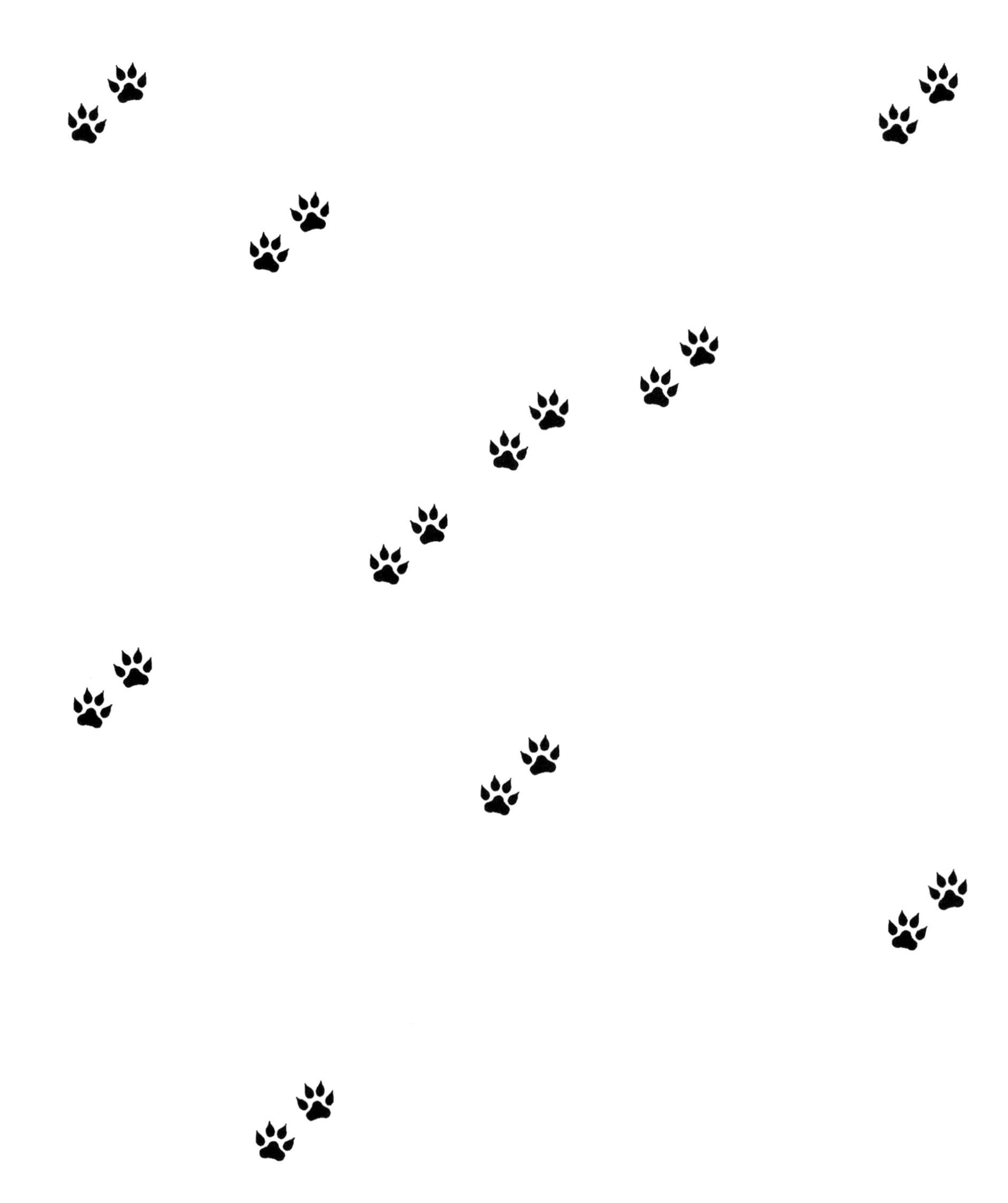

PART 2
RAISING YOUR PUPPY

CARING FOR YOUR PUPPY

How much should I feed my puppy? What vaccinations does my puppy need? And what equipment should I buy? These are typical of the many questions new puppy owners have.

FEEDING

All 20+ of Adobe's veterinarians seem to agree that most people overfeed their puppies. It's easy to do, especially when they eat as fast as Labs. Many Lab and Golden puppies don't really seem to eat; it's much more like they vacuum the food into their stomachs. It's not natural for dogs to have their food come to them in a bowl and most puppies do eat way too fast. You can slow them down by feeding them in a larger area (like the back lawn or the whole kitchen floor) or by putting a plate or LARGE river rock in his food bowl, or by feeding from one of the many new toys available for dispensing treats and food. If you choose the rock method, it's imperative that the rock be WAY too large for him to eat, even as an adult.

As for foods, the amount on the back of the bag is WRONG! ALWAYS. Most of us are feeding very high quality, highly digestible foods that are very calorie-dense. What all of those terms mean is you need to feed far less for your pup to get the right amount of nutrition. If a puppy is having more than three bowel movements a day, he is almost certainly eating too much. If his stool is loose or paste-like, he is probably eating too much. If he has a cute, hanging belly more than 2 hours after eating, he's eating too

much. If you can't EASILY feel, with the flat of your hand, his ribs, just behind his shoulders (yes, he has ribs there) he's eating too much. Why care? Well, dogs that are fat as puppies are far more prone to crippling orthopedic problems as they mature. Everything from painful "growing pains" to bones that form pieces that break off into their joints requiring expensive and invasive surgery. It also makes housetraining more difficult and can make all training more challenging.

Large breeds should be fed a low protein food (24% or less) to discourage rapid growth, which can result in the same painful conditions mentioned above in addition to increased incidents of Hip and Elbow Dysplasia. It's much better to keep your puppy lean than to take the chance that he could be crippled permanently because of too much food.

It's impossible to say exactly how much a puppy should eat. But every few weeks, they need to eat more. Puppies grow astonishingly fast. They will often double their weight from 8 to 12 weeks and then again from 16 weeks to maturity. A lean puppy is not the same as a thin puppy. Make sure your puppy is gaining weight appropriately and that you increase his food volume in proportion to his weight gain.

Here are some VERY general feeding guidelines for VERY average puppies. Remember that the number of calories in the food you are feeding will change the amount you feed. The amounts below are based on an average dog food with approximately 350 k/cal per cup. This information is often NOT on the bag of food. You may have to call the manufacturer's "800" number to find out how many calories per cup of your puppy's food.

A 16-week-old, four pound Pomeranian puppy should be eating two tablespoons or so of a good quality dog food two to three times per day. This puppy, at eight weeks, probably ate a tablespoon per feeding.

An eight-week-old Lab or Golden puppy should be getting a half cup or so of adult dog or large breed puppy food three times a day. The same puppy, at 12 weeks may be getting three-quarters of a cup of food two to three times a day and at 20 weeks probably close to three cups of food total per day in two feedings.

A six-pound, eight-week-old puppy could be getting one-quarter to one-third of a cup of food per day; the difference would be that a pudgy puppy would get the lower end of the scale.

A Mastiff puppy at 16 weeks old may be getting three cups of large breed puppy food or adult dog food per day. There is evidence that breaking this into three meals per day may reduce the chances of him getting Bloat (see below) later in life.

The most important thing is that if you have worries that your puppy is getting too thin, feed more! Then ask your vet right away. Keep your puppy healthy and sound by keeping him lean and fit. Remember that most of your neighbors have no idea what a healthy weight looks like; they may tell you your puppy is too thin, but trust your vet. At our practice, as many as eight out of ten dogs we see are moderately to severely overweight and many of their owners aren't even aware of it!

BLOAT

Bloat (Gastric Dilation Volvulus) is when a dog's stomach swells with food or gas then flips over, twisting and sealing off the intestine and esophagus so nothing can get in or out. The stomach will continue to swell, stretching blood vessels so tightly that blood flow is dangerously restricted. If untreated within a couple of hours, the result is often fatal.

Bloat is a condition most often seen in large, deep-chested, narrow-waisted dogs like Irish Setters, Standard Poodles, German Shepherds, and Great Danes. It is most common in dogs over four years old and the risk increases with each year of age. Bloat is included in here because the way a puppy is fed MAY affect his risk of bloating as an adult. It is important to avoid feeding large meals to a puppy of a breed that may be at risk. Talk to your vet if you are unsure about your puppy's future risk. We don't know exactly what causes Bloat but when it happens it is life threatening in a very short time.

New research indicates that feeding dogs large meals once a day may contribute to the chance of Bloat by stretching the ligaments that support the stomach. Exercising with a full stomach may cause the same thing. We know that Bloat is more common during stress like thunderstorms or Fourth of July fireworks. We have learned that feeding a dog from an elevated platform will INCREASE the risk of Bloat. If you have more questions, speak with your vet.

PARASITES AND DEWORMING

Many vets are divided on the subject of deworming with possibly the biggest divisions being geographic. Some feel that it shouldn't be done unless a stool sample tests positive and some feel it is imperative to deworm all puppies routinely. The Centers for Disease Control (CDC) recommends a deworming schedule that is frequent and thorough. Many of the parasites found in most of the country can be communicated to humans (especially children) and the CDC's job is to protect people.

If your puppy has worms, they should be able to be identified by a tech looking at a prepared sample under a microscope. In my area (the San Francisco Bay Area) we most commonly see roundworms and coccidian. Other parasites that affect puppies in the Bay Area are tapeworms (from eating an infected flea), giardia (from contaminated water or wildlife/livestock), and spirochetes (usually just an upset in the balance of the flora of the gut). Most of the parasites that cause diarrhea are NOT visible on a routine microscopic stool screening. If your puppy has diarrhea, talk with your vet before bringing a stool sample, as he or she will probably need to make a special slide to look for the little beasts that cause it.

Tapeworms and roundworms can be visible to the naked eye. Tapeworms look like little grains of rice and may be visible ON fresh stool. Maggots are often confused with tapeworms by pet owners but are NOT a parasite of the dog's GI system. Maggots are IN the stool that has been on the ground for a couple of hours and tapeworms, again, are ON fresh stool. Tapeworms can also stick to the hair around the dog's bottom and may dry to tiny, yellow-to-brown-dried-out-ricey-looking things. Roundworms are long, thin, spaghetti-looking things that may be visible in stool or vomit. Neither worm is a huge deal to the puppy. It is NOT an emergency. It's really gross, but not an emergency.

Vaccinations

All puppies need to be vaccinated against Distemper and Parvovirus. UC Davis recommends that these vaccines be given at 6-8, 9-11, and 12-16 weeks of age. While some puppies may attain immunity at 12 weeks, the vets at Adobe agree that it is safest for most puppies to be treated as though their immunity is incomplete until they have received their final puppy vaccine at 16 weeks.

Parvo is a virus that can affect all dogs but puppies are at the greatest risk. It causes severe diarrhea, lethargy, lack of appetite, and vomiting. Without aggressive treatment it is almost always fatal; even with treatment, some puppies may die. Parvo can live in dirt for years and a puppy can get it just by walking through a contaminated area. For this reason, we recommend your puppy not be taken to unpaved public areas until his immunity is complete. Avoid schoolyards, dog parks, and fields that other dogs frequent. When you take your puppy for a walk, keep him away from areas where other dogs go potty. It's also critical that you keep him away from dogs that have recently been in a shelter or a boarding kennel, or a puppy that has been shipped in from anywhere.

Distemper has nothing to do with your puppy's personality. It is not a "temperament shot" as many people believe. The Distemper vaccine is usually given as a "combo" with up to seven other vaccines in one shot. Distemper is a virus that is spread through the air, like a cold. It is a very bad disease that is usually fatal and even if puppies live through it, they often have physical problems from it for the rest of their lives. Early symptoms of Distemper often look like Kennel Cough but are usually much more severe. It often progresses from cold-like symptoms to twitching and/or diarrhea.

Even puppies with incomplete immunity are in need of socialization; we recommend that once your pup has had his second set of vaccines or at 10 weeks old (depending on your vet's comfort level) you start taking him places to meet people and well cared for dogs. Walking your downtown area is good as are many malls. I recommend finding a home improvement store or video store that will welcome your little social butterfly. The more people, noises, and sights you can expose him to at this young age, the better.

Once a puppy has completed the series of vaccines, he won't need another vaccine for a year from the last vaccine. Vaccine protocols vary by veterinarian and geographical area. Generally, Distemper, Parvo, and Rabies vaccines have been determined to protect adult dogs for at least three years. You should expect to repeat your pup's 16 week vaccines at 16 months, then every three years after that. Adobe does NOT recommend yearly vaccinations (with rare exceptions).

`A Rabies vaccine can be given after your puppy is 12 to 16 weeks old, depending on state laws. Once he has been vaccinated he can be licensed with your city animal control. You should ask them if waiting to license until after your pet is spayed or neutered is beneficial. Many cities offer substantially lower fees for altered pets.

If your puppy will be exposed to livestock or areas frequented by wild mammals (including Sea Lions), you should discuss the Leptospirosis vaccine with your vet. Leptospirosis is an often-deadly disease that can be communicated to humans. This vaccine should be given only to dogs over 12 weeks of age, as it has been associated with more severe post vaccine reactions (including anaphylaxis) than other vaccines. Adobe only uses the vaccine most likely to cover the strains found in our area. We NEVER recommend it as part of a "combo" vaccine. Most suburban dogs should not receive this vaccine but hunting dogs and ranch dogs are at higher risk and should be vaccinated before the rainy season. The vaccine is 50-75% effective, but in a disease like this, every little bit helps. This vaccine WILL require yearly boosters if the dog's lifestyle remains the same.

Corona is commonly found in combo vaccines and should only be given to dogs constantly exposed to a wide variety of dogs from a wide variety of geographic regions.

Giardia, Lymes, and rattlesnake venom vaccines need to be carefully evaluated for effectiveness and safety. Giardia, for instance, is an easily treated disease, affecting very few dogs in general. We feel that this is overkill and not appropriate for our patients.***

HEARTWORM PREVENTION

Adobe ran a low-cost screening for Heartworm Disease (HWD) in the winter of 2004. We are at the southern tip of the San Francisco Bay and have not seen heartworms be a big problem. We wanted to make sure things had not changed, so we ran over 400 Heartworm tests, mostly on dogs and cats we considered at higher risk. For example, dogs NOT on a preventative and living in areas with documented cases of HWD in Coyotes. In all of the testing, we came up with one positive. One. And that dog came to the Bay Area from a known heartworm area in the Sierra foothills. Our conclusion has to be that while we can't guarantee it will never be a problem, it's not a problem right now.

That said, if your dog is the one to get the rare case of HWD in this area, your dog has a very serious, life threatening disease that requires expensive, serious, and dangerous treatment and it could have been prevented by giving a simple, safe treatment once a month. We know that HWD is getting closer. We see occasional cases. It's a completely preventable disease.

Some important things to know about HWD:

- It's transmitted in the bite of a certain type of mosquito.
- The mosquito MUST have already bitten an infected animal to transmit it.
- It takes six months after infection to show up on a test. If you miss a month and you're nervous, continue the preventative and test in six months.
- The heartworm preventative actually works to kill the baby worms your dog was exposed to in the month BEFORE you give the preventative. In other words, it doesn't do any good to give the preventative before you go to an active HW area. You need to give it afterward, so it can kill any of the little buggers that got in there.
- Some Collies are sensitive to large amounts of the active ingredients in Heartworm preventatives. If you have a Collie or Collie-type dog be sure to discuss the best preventative with your vet.

FLEAS AND TICKS

Ah...not much can compare to the passion we feel about keeping fleas off our pets and out of our homes. Back in the olden days we used lots of horrible and dangerous chemicals and we still couldn't beat the little beasts! Now we have very safe and effective chemicals and most of the time, we beat them!

There are many products on the market, which work well, when used correctly. Advantage and Frontline are excellent and may be purchased over-the-counter, which means no prescription is needed. Revolution is a great product that is a dewormer, flea and tick control, and heartworm preventative. It is different from the others because it is FDA approved, making it a drug, not a pesticide. This product is available by prescription only.

At the time of this writing, all monthly flea and tick control products take up to 48 hours to kill ticks. Unfortunately, that's plenty of time for tick-borne illnesses to be transmitted to your dog. The only product I'm aware of that actually prevents ticks from biting is the Preventic collar. It must be used strictly as the instructions state, but it works for three months and paralyzes ticks when they get on your dog. I recommend this prevention if your dog will be exposed to ticks.

MEDS BY MAIL

There are lots of places you can buy your pet's medications by mail. A lot of them advertise low, low prices. I recommend asking your vet if they will match the price you'd pay online. Most of them would rather keep your business in-house and will be happy to meet the price.

EXERCISE

All puppies need lots of exercise. Left to their own, they would play and explore for 30 or 40 minutes, then collapse and take a nap. Then they wake up and go potty, and start the whole cycle over again. Your puppy needs naps, too. Otherwise you'll end up with a crazy, destructive, and hyper puppy.

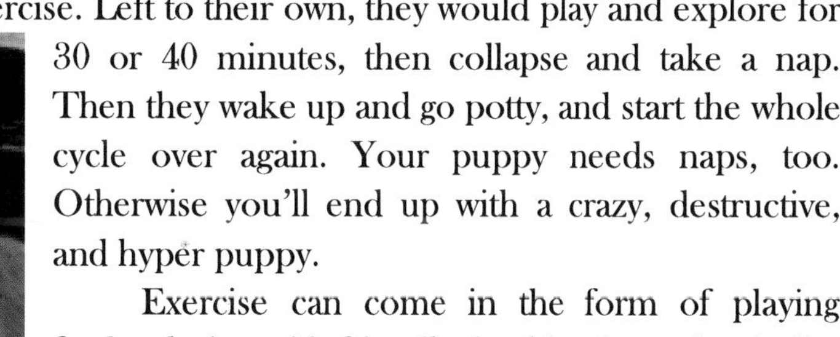

Exercise can come in the form of playing fetch, playing with friendly, healthy dogs of a similar size, swimming, gentle jogging, and leash walking. No puppy should be let off leash in an unconfined area until he is old enough to know not to lose you and to come to you if he gets frightened. Many puppies run away when they're scared and that can be very dangerous.

For large and giant breed puppies, exercise should be steady and mostly straight lines. No quick turns and spins. Make sure most of their footing provides good traction so they can keep their feet under them. Don't let big puppies jump from trucks without you supporting their landing. This may help prevent some elbow and shoulder injuries.

Training

All puppies need training. The sooner the better! We encourage all puppy owners to sign up for a puppy socialization class as soon as they know they're getting a puppy. Puppies will be welcomed into class as young as 10 weeks of age. Puppies over 18 weeks at the start of class will be too old. It's a very short window of opportunity and it's critical to use this time to our best advantage.

Good puppy classes are really socialization classes for the puppies. They need to learn that there are dogs of all shapes and sizes and that while they may look different, the social rules still apply. Puppies in these classes will continue to perfect their bite inhibition skills and learn to speak "dog" more fluently. You will learn more about housetraining, manners, and typical puppy raising problems. It's a great way to catch behavior problems early and figure out the best way to address them. I often laugh that it's more of a class for people than puppies! Sort of a support group for new puppy owners.

Grooming

All puppies need grooming. Whether they have long hair or short, they all need to learn to accept being groomed. Most puppies do best if you start them with a baby (human) brush. These brushes are very soft, won't pull long or curly hair, and won't scratch skin. MOST puppies will try to bite the brush as if it's a toy and may get your hand in the process.

One really easy way to make your puppy behave and be still is to give him or her something wonderful to eat like some peanut butter or low fat cream cheese smeared very thinly on a plate. Let your puppy start licking the peanut butter and if she turns to bite the brush, take the peanut butter and yourself away. Try again in a minute or so. A few repetitions are all it will take to keep her attention on her peanut butter and off of the brush. When she is getting really good at it, start giving her the peanut butter after a minute or two of brushing. Start making the peanut butter appear later and later in the session. Your puppy should learn that being polite and patient will pay off.

Playing with your pup's feet is a critical part of puppy training and grooming. Every day, you should handle your pup's feet and look for stickers, burrs, gum, tar, and mats. You need to look between the toes and in the bottom of the feet in the space around the large foot pad. Any swelling, odor, or discharge should be addressed with your vet immediately. Nails can be inspected at this point, too. I recommend new puppy owners use a nail file instead of nail trimmers. Nail trimmers can be scary for both puppy and owner. You can get great results with a nail file.

TOYS AND CHEWS

Puppies start teething about the same time they start learning to play, at about three-and-a-half weeks old. Play may look like chewing sometimes and chewing may resemble play, but chewing is serious business for your puppy. Dogs chew as a form of stress relief, pain relief, and to help their big, giant teeth stay healthy. ALL puppies need something to chew on. Chewies are for chewing. Toys don't count as chewies. A chewie needs to be able to fit into the very back of their mouth, to give relief to those moving molars. It needs to be exciting enough to keep the puppy (or dog) chewing for an extended period. It should encourage the use of ALL parts of the mouth, including the tiny little incisors at the very front of his mouth. A puppy who chews every day will be a healthier dog for it, both mentally and physically!

Appropriate chewies include rawhide, raw beef bones, "bully sticks," and pig ears for delicate chewers. Some dogs like bone-like plastic or nylon bones but I don't think

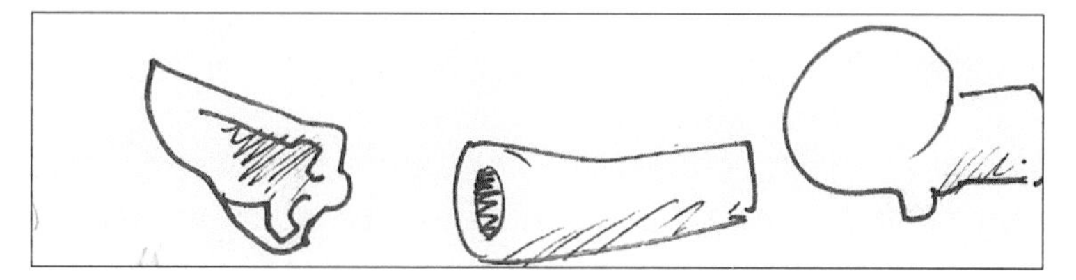

there is a substitute as good as the real thing. Raw beef bones are great for puppies and dogs. I get mine from the butcher, keep them in the freezer, and give them to my dogs frozen in the summer. Frozen bones are also soothing for puppy's mouths. Cooked, smoked, and otherwise processed bones are harder and more brittle.

Ham bones, lamb bones, and other bones available in pet stores may be very high in fat in addition to being brittle and easily splintered. We don't recommend these, at all. Your cooked steak, ham, or lamb leg could easily splinter and cause disastrous results. Chewies should be allowed in excess. It's fine for your dog to be working on three or four different types.

Toys are for playing! There are the most amazing toys available, choose the ones that make sense to you. Rope toys are great for tug-of-war, balls are great for chasing, and

squeaky, plush toys are fun for one-on-one *supervised* play. I don't recommend that most dogs have unlimited access to plush toys because they're easy to tear up. It's a very small step from a plush toy to a pillow to a couch. Puppies are too young to know the difference. Keep the plush toys in a special place and don't give unsupervised access. That said there are some dogs that will never destroy a toy. If you have one of those, it's ok to allow a little more time with the toy, unless he proves you wrong!

COLLARS AND LEASHES

Puppies do best on regular old buckle or snap collars. Most puppies will pull backwards and buck like a bronco when they are first learning to walk on a leash, so you need to fit it snugly and check it every week. Puppies grow so fast! Their collars can quickly become dangerously tight. Always choose the lightest weight, narrowest leash and collar with the lightest weight hardware you safely can. I see tiny puppies carrying around giant collars and leashes with snaps that could hold a horse! Our goal will be to never need anything heavier than a three-quarter-inch wide leather leash, no matter how big the dog! We get there with *training*, not restraining.

Harnesses are not something I recommend, with the exception of the Easy Walk Harness. It was designed with the leash snapping onto the front of the harness, not the back. Most dogs just stop pulling. I don't really know why, but it works.

I don't recommend choke-type collars at all anymore. If your dog needs more than the Easy Walk Harness or a flat collar, a more humane option is the prong or pinch collar. This collar should not be needed on a puppy younger than five months old. It's pretty common that breeds like Labs, Goldens, Rotts, and Pit Bulls need a little extra help making good decisions about walking on a leash. They have been bred, in large part, not to pay much attention to minor discomforts and to do whatever it takes to get what they want. So sometimes, it's important for them to get a very clear signal about right and wrong. Pinch collars need to be fitted precisely and used with close attention, otherwise they are just abusive. They should only be used with an experienced trainer's guidance. This doesn't mean you always have to have a trainer with you; rather, you just need to learn the rules.

Head halter-type "collars" have been very popular in that past few years. They go around the dog's muzzle, giving you control of the head. The problem is that some dogs HATE having anything on their face and will fight it. The other problem is that some dogs are too sensitive for it and will cower. Some dogs do great with them and I will recommend them in some circumstances, but not usually on a young puppy.

So go with a properly fitted buckle collar or an Easy Walk Harness and a lightweight, comfortable leash. If you develop problems along the way, buy the proper tool at that time. This is not an area to economize.

THE LONG RUN

This guide should help you get through the early months. Get a good trainer and use her/him. Most dogs are "rehomed" (gotten rid of) between five and 24 months. That's when their adolescence makes their owners think they are "bad dogs." Be patient and consistent and ask for help if you need it. Dogs that have never been "bad" a day in their lives can act like maniacs all of a sudden in adolescence. Don't worry. Increase exercise and supervision and work with your trainer. Your puppy will grow out of it. Keep working, and have fun. You'll end up with your perfect dog.

PUPPY POINTERS

Puppies! Oh how we love them! But we hate their sharp teeth and our loss of sleep and the stains on the carpet. But most of all, we hate not knowing what to do with them. We hear so many conflicting instructions. I'm going to try to address some of the most common issues and give some good solid answers. In the process, your puppy will grow up healthy, happy, well socialized and a joy to be around. Eventually, your puppy *will* be a joy to be around, but there are a lot of stages between now and then.

Remember that, even though your puppy will look all grown up within a few months, he'll be a puppy until anywhere from nine months (tiny, toy breeds) to two-and-a-half years old (bigger, slower growing breeds). He'll still need you to look out for him and keep him safe from himself. He'll need to be reminded about some really basic rules off and on between now and then. And he'll need your love and understanding to make sure you don't have to "get rid of him." Remember that if you live with a dog, you are always teaching him something. Whether it's something good or something bad is up to you.

All puppies are in homes where they are loved at first. As they grow and mature, they become incorrigible at times. This is normal. Unfortunately, most puppy owners are not prepared for it and thousands of formerly loved puppies end up in shelters or new homes where they will never fulfill their promise. In these next pages I hope to prepare you for the worst and help you encourage the best from your pup. I hope to open the door to training so that when something comes up, you know where to go for answers and how to get them soon enough to thwart any serious problems.

Biting

Biting is a puppy's way of learning. Just as human babies learn to use their hands by gripping a toy or dad's finger, puppies learn about grip, too. They grip with their mouths. Unfortunately, puppies have relatively weak jaws so Mother Nature equipped them with super sharp teeth to enable them to eat. Outside the care of humans, puppies are expected to eat what Mom brings them, raw meat. And Mother Nature did a great job on those teeth, didn't she?! The teeth are designed to hold and tear flesh. They are designed to stab right through the tough hide of an animal so the puppy can carry away a piece of meat bigger than itself without losing it. And they WORK!

Your challenge is to teach your puppy to control those teeth. This is a natural extension of what he would be learning had he stayed with his littermates. In fact, this training has already begun provided your puppy stayed in contact with his mom and siblings until he was at least seven weeks old. See, mom and the kids don't like the feel of his teeth either. So in the middle of an exciting game of wrestling, if he bit too hard or with too much enthusiasm, they would yelp and turn away. The play would stop. So he started to learn to control his bite. People have much more wimpy skin than puppies so you need to be ready to continue the training. It works best to adopt the method of training he's used to.

It's as important NOT to do certain things as it is to do things a certain way. Grabbing your pup's muzzle won't work. It almost always causes an escalation in biting. The pup is playing and you were playing and now you're being scary with the muzzle grab, so he gets scared and wants to tell you off. He thinks that you want to play more roughly! So he bites harder and faster and gets out of the danger zone (arm's reach) fast! Yelling, "NO!" and grabbing him, is also really confusing and can cause a puppy not to trust you and to stay out of arm's reach. However, it doesn't teach them how hard is too hard to bite.

Alternatively, if you use the following instructions, you should have a puppy that isn't using his mouth on you, by the time he's 18 weeks old. He will know how hard is too hard and how to play with people.

When your puppy is playing with you and his teeth hurt, YELP, "OUCH!"! Then fold your arms and freeze. Act like it hurt. Some puppies will start looking more ferocious and will bark and act like they're going to bite again. Some actually WILL bite you again, and will look scary when they do it. The key is that almost 100% of puppies will do it much more softly than the bite that made you yelp. Some of them may actually just bump you with their jaw. This is GREAT! This means that they get it and that they will start using their mouth much more softly. *It's important to yelp only at the bites that actually do hurt in the beginning.* He needs to learn to control his teeth, not just "don't use them." Later, you'll want to yelp at only the hardest bites. Your puppy will probably regress off and on until he's 5 months old or so, so be prepared to give a really convincing yelp for those "just checking" bites.

If your puppy is not impressed that you yelped and froze and he bites you again and this bite is HARDER that the one that made you yelp, put him in his crate. *Immediately.* He's probably overtired and/or over-stimulated and is crazy. Let him take a nap, then go right back to what you were doing and if he goes back to biting, start with the yelp again. If he really doesn't care that he hurt you, and bites harder, and you have made sure that he's not over stimulated or tired, you should call a good trainer to come and help you. Continue to crate him for biting.

Most dogs get this very quickly. To teach him not to mouth people at all, gradually accept less and less pressure until his teeth touching your skin makes you yelp. He will learn that people really *are* wimps and will be very careful in the future. This is called bite inhibition and it's very important to his future. If he is injured or in pain and someone tries to move him, that person is at much less risk of being badly bitten than by a dog without good bite inhibition. A dog without bite inhibition thinks he has to bite much harder to get his point across and can cause serious damage.

If a puppy takes food too roughly, it's almost always because you experienced how sharp his tiny teeth are, and now you unconsciously pull your hand back a bit just before he gets the treat. He then grabs for the treat, thinking that he's going to lose it. The cure for this, believe it or not, is to hide the treat in the tips of your fingers and thumb and *push* your hand toward his mouth. Not into his mouth, just a long smooth movement toward his mouth. It will surprise him because he's used to having to grab it. He doesn't want your fingers, he wants the treat, and so he'll try to work past your fingers and will lick to find the treat at the same time. When he licks your fingers, give the treat.

As your confidence builds, start giving the treat like a normal person and remember he gets it when he licks your hand.

If that doesn't work, YELP loudly and take the food away. Try again as described above and repeat the yelping as needed.

If he becomes overexcited and rude, close your hands, fold your arms against your chest, and look up, away from him. Make sure the message is clear, "the candy store is closed!" Shut down until he backs off. Do not push him off with your hands and be sure to say nothing. When he sits in front of you or gives up and wanders off, try again and continue to insist that he take treats gently. He should get it quickly and be fine.

I don't approve of giving a verbal command like *gentle* or *be nice.* Giving a command insinuates that there are times he might not need to be gentle or nice. It is a requirement of life that he ALWAYS be polite when taking treats. He will absolutely learn this without a verbal instruction.

CRATE TRAINING

I recommend crate training your pup. A crate is a safe and secure place for your puppy to be when he's not with you. Its use is similar to that of a crib or a playpen for a human baby. I recommend the wire fold down crates as they are very versatile and your puppy will have a clear view of the household. The crate should be placed where your puppy can see the family going about their business. He should feel a part of the family, not isolated. Locking your dog in a room with the door closed is a surefire way to cause screaming and yelling and fear. Your puppy needs to know that he's still at home, and being all alone on the other side of a door is scary.

To teach your puppy how great a crate is, teach him the trick, *kennel.* Stand or kneel outside the crate with some incredible treats. Toss one or two just inside and say *kennel* in a cheerful voice. When the puppy puts any part of his body in the crate to get the treat tell him, "good!" and give him another treat from your hand. Ask him to go inside farther and farther until he's inside looking at you. Then give him a jackpot! A jackpot is just what it sounds like. An exciting increase in the number of treats he gets, out of the blue. When he's finished with the treats call him out of the crate and ignore him for a few minutes; you want him to get attention for going IN, not coming out.

Now take a step back from the crate and ask him to *kennel.* Start dropping treats through the top of the crate while he's in there. Each time, *call* him out and send him back in. When he's in the crate, start waiting a second or two before running over and giving him his treat. *Only give the treat if he's still in the crate when you get there.* Start sending him from farther and farther away until you can get him to go there from all over the house. Continue to wait a little longer each time to take him his treat. Secure a bone and an indestructible toy inside the crate so they are always there when he gets there. When he's very comfortable going into his crate and happily waiting to be called out of it, give him an irresistible chewy and close the door of the crate. The second he starts to chew on the chewy, open the crate and call him out. Lure him with a treat if necessary, but get him out of the crate. Of course, the chewy stays in...you want him to really want that chewy! You want him to beg you to say *kennel.* While he's obviously distracted by the chewy, send him back in. When he gets started, call him out again. Yes, we want him to want you to leave him alone in his crate so he can chew on the chewy! That's your job. Don't call him out so often that he gets frustrated, but keep reminding him how great the crate is. Soon you can start increasing the amount of time he spends in there.

How long can my puppy stay in his crate? THE RULE OF THUMB IS 1 HOUR PER MONTH OF AGE, PLUS 1 HOUR but never longer than 8 hours, even for an adult dog. So a three-month-old puppy can spend up to four hours at a time in the crate. During the daytime. At night, most puppies can go at least six hours. I believe that all puppies under 16 weeks need to be sound asleep by 9:00 P.M. Wake them up to go potty at 11:00 P.M. and then they should sleep 'til sixish. Puppies do best sleeping in your bedroom at night.

HOUSETRAINING

Housetraining is hard. It's not something that dogs really understand. Dogs just don't care. I know we always hear that dogs want to keep their den clean. They do...but have you seen how big a den for a dog is? It's tiny! Our houses are just plain crazy to them! Lie down on your floor so your eyes are at your puppy's eyelevel and look around. YOU LIVE IN A FOREST! Why on earth would people care where a tiny bit of poo or pee is? Dogs don't get it. They have to learn to care because you care. Once they get it, it works pretty well. Your job is to make sure you remember how ridiculous it is to your dog. Just keep it in perspective.

Step 1: Confinement

Your puppy has to be confined somewhere at times. That's just the way it is. Sorry, no way around it. I recommend a crate or two. Some pups do fine with a crate large enough for them to be in when they're adults but some puppies will go potty in them. If your puppy is one of the latter, buy a smaller crate. A much smaller crate. Don't fight it, just do it. It will save you time and money and frustration later. A large crate will be seen by some puppies as a bedroom *and* a bathroom and they will potty in the part they're not sleeping in.

Step 2: Schedule

The BEST way to housetrain a puppy is NEVER to let him go potty in the house. That is definitely easier said than done. When your pup has been in the crate for a couple of hours (napping and chewing on a fabulous chewy) take him outside to go potty ON LEASH. Stand and wait and ignore him. Plan on waiting up to five minutes with him. Say *go potty* or whatever your cue will be quietly and softly. If he goes potty, say, "gooooooooooood" in the same soft voice. Don't startle him by praising loudly or suddenly. As he's having a bowel movement and/or urinating tell him what a good puppy he is and pop a treat into his mouth! Then take him inside to play. Remember that when puppies are playing hard, they need to go potty every 20 to 30 minutes, so make sure to put him back in his crate or take him out in plenty of time.

He should stay in his crate for a couple of hours, and then repeat the trip outside. Don't feel mean, puppies need lots of naps. It's best for your puppy to nap in his crate where he's safe and he doesn't feel the need to follow you from room to room.

If he didn't go potty during the five minutes, he should go back into his crate for 30 minutes, and then you can try again. If he still doesn't go, back into the crate for 15-30 minutes. Try again. Keep this schedule until he's gone potty. When he really has to go, this strategy will work to your benefit because *it feels good to relieve yourself when you really have to go.* That will be part of his reward. The other part is getting to play in the yard with you! Take a minute to really play with him; make sure you don't play with him before he goes potty. He should go potty fast to get it out of the way and to earn his treat and play session. If you take him back in immediately after going potty, he'll figure out that the longer he "holds it," the longer he gets to stay outside!

A good schedule for most households is roughly as follows:

7:00-8:00 A.M. take your puppy outside to go potty.

If he goes...feed and water him.

10 to 20 minutes later...take him outside again.

If he goes...playtime.

If not...back into the crate as above.

11:00A.M.-Noon back outside to go potty.

Feed and water puppies under 16 weeks old.

If your puppy was fed...10 to 20 minutes later take him outside.

If your puppy was not fed...playtime.

4:00-5:00 P,M, outside to go potty, water.

7:00 P.M. feed and water your puppy.

10-20 minutes later outside to go potty.

11:00 P.M. outside to go potty. Even if he's asleep. Just wake him and take him out (emphasis on TAKE him out).

When he goes potty, praise quietly and back inside to bed. No playing, no treats, no loud praise. Just back to bed.

Most puppies will make it to at least 6:00 A.M.. Try to start extending the nighttime to 7:00 or 8:00 A.M. or whatever your family's normal schedule is.

STEP 3: DEALING WITH ACCIDENTS

As the popular saying goes, "accidents happen." Ok, that's my version of the popular saying. But it's true. You are human and your puppy is bound to have an accident or two. The thing to keep in mind is that *each accident your puppy has in the house costs you weeks in house training.* Really. You probably know that you're not supposed to punish your dog unless you catch him in the act but be careful what you're punishing him for! If you scold your puppy because you catch him going potty in the house, in your puppy's brain you are scolding him for going potty in front of you! It doesn't have anything to do with the house because puppies don't get the whole "house" concept. They just know that you saw them going potty and you were MAD! So next time, they'll be a lot less likely to go potty in front of you.

"GOOD" you say! Isn't that the point? No, if your puppy doesn't want to go potty in front of you, it makes him much harder to housetrain because he won't go potty as easily when you take him out. Worse than that, it makes it much more likely that he'll hide under a table or in the closet to go potty so you won't have to see. "What could be bad about that?" says his cute, little pea brain. You don't walk in the closet or behind the couch, so, to him, that's a perfect answer. Because you haven't taught him never to go potty in the house.

Next time your puppy has an accident in the house, get the biggest, heaviest newspaper you can find and roll it up tightly. Take it into the bathroom, look in the mirror and whack yourself over the head, scolding, "Bad Owner! BAD, BAD

OWNER!" because if there's an accident, it's not your puppy's fault, it's yours. Make sure the puppy is confined when you can't watch him and take him out often enough.

To clean up accident sites, use an enzymatic cleanser like Natures Miracle. If the puppy is (politely) having his accidents in a little used area, like in front of the TV or on a far corner of a room, clean it well and then lie down there and read a book while you let him hang out with you on his leash and chew a chewy. Soon, that's not a little used place anymore! That works all over the house. A little used area is anything off of your most commonly used paths. Your puppy has nothing to do all day but watch you...closely. He can tell within inches what your normal routes through the house are. If you look at where puppy is pottying, it's probably just off of the spaces you actually walk on. Pretty interesting, isn't it?

STEP 4: GETTING THROUGH THE 16TH WEEK

Most puppies, as they hit 16 weeks of age, regress in their training. All training. You may get an accident or two, or you may get a puppy that looks at you like you're from another planet, when you say *sit!* Don't worry; you haven't done anything wrong. Puppies go through a hormonal change at that age and it seems to affect their training. Just stay consistent and everything will be back to normal in a week or so.

STEP 5: IS HE HOUSETRAINED YET?

Another rule of thumb is that a puppy needs to be accident free for a minimum of six weeks (some behaviorists say six months!!) and at least six months old to be considered housetrained. That doesn't mean you can go out and leave him unsupervised; it means he's good about not going potty in the house. The great majority of puppies don't seem to have the mental maturity to "ask" to go outside until they are at least six months old. Until then, supervise and manage.

POSSESSED PUPPY SYNDROME

Most owners of young puppies report that the pup goes crazy as often as four times per day. Really crazy. For some pups it may be as mild as running laps around the house like a wild thing. For some it might be jumping and biting at faces or ears or acting like he's possessed. The times most commonly reported are within a couple of hours of getting up in the morning, around lunchtime, around four in the afternoon, and around seven at night. The other common denominator is that the puppy "won't listen" during these times. He is WILD. If you've had small children you've probably seen the same kind of behavior in them. It's a manifestation of being over-stimulated and overtired.

Young puppies need to sleep A LOT and our lifestyles are often not conducive to that. And they become sleep deprived. Pups that are eight weeks old often sleep more than they're awake if left with their litter. But when they live in our homes they often put off sleep in favor of PLAY. As your pup gets older his sleep requirements will decrease. But he still needs naps, just like a baby (he IS a baby!). Make sure your pup gets plenty of time and encouragement to nap. Most puppies need 18-20 hours of sleep a day!

DO NOT try to discipline or reason with your puppy when he's suffering from Possessed Puppy Syndrome! It will do nothing but frustrate you and inflame the problem, which could lead to your puppy worrying about whether or not he should trust you. Instead, pick him up gently, take him to his crate, and tell him, "poor puppy...you're insane with tiredness...you go to sleep now" (or something else sympathetic). And leave him in there for at least an hour. This is not to punish him, but to give him time to sleep.

TOLERANCE

Teaching your puppy to tolerate humanisms is a very important part of having a dog. It is very important that you teach him to accept people doing all kinds of crazy (in his mind) things to him. You and your vet and groomer and even total strangers should be able to touch him everywhere without struggle.

As a baby, your puppy should have already been exposed to people touching his feet and ears and tail. You need to continue that training and add restraint in different forms. Hugging your dog is actually a form of restraint and you can modify it to make it very versatile. You also need to teach him to allow his feet to be held and his tail held and moved. He must allow his ears to be held and looked into and he must allow a stranger to hover over him and hold his legs and head. All of these are things that will happen at the vet or the groomer and it's not fair not to prepare your pup for them.

The Magic Puppy Hold really is magic. It calms puppies and puts them in a slower frame of mind. It teaches them to tolerate restraint and it helps us learn about a behavior/temperament problem that may be bubbling just beneath the surface. I recommend that people use this hold several times a day and that parents help children learn to do it too.

Sitting in a chair (cross-legged on the floor works better for large puppies), hold your puppy facing away from you. His spine should be in line with yours, exactly in the middle of your chest. Tuck your left hand under his bottom with your palm between his hind legs on the very low part of his belly and your fingers close to your belly. Tuck him in pretty securely. Your right hand should gently CUP his muzzle and keep it facing straight away from you. Do not grip his muzzle; this will cause panic and that's not what we want. He will probably struggle to free himself. Some puppies might cry and throw a fit. Just hang on and insist that he allows himself to be restrained. Believe me, it's much better for you to teach this at home than have it happen at the vet or groomer. Hold him until he relaxes, talking to him in a soothing, loving voice, then put him down to play.

You should practice this hold often—at least four or five times a day, until your puppy just melts. Have strangers do it too. Again, this is something that is almost cruel to ignore. If your puppy goes to the vet and needs to be held still for something and won't, they just keep adding techs to hold him down until he either can't move or gives up. This is something you really need to teach your dog.

COME

Everybody wants their dog to *come* "on command." The problem is that we do so many things to convince them not to! Most people use the word *come* as a generic correction. I have seen people tell their dog to *come* when they want him out of the trash or off the couch or away from another dog. It seems to be human nature. Well, you might wonder, what's wrong with calling your dog? If you use *come* to call your dog from something interesting, it's just another sound to ignore. We are talking about a baby. He needs a good, positive start to figure out why he should do what people want.

I find that most people who yell, "Rover, *Come*!" haven't taught the puppy what *come* means. I think of it as yelling, "Do Calculus!" at a four-year-old child; you can yell it as loudly as you like, but if they don't know what to do, they don't know what to do!

It's critical that you teach your puppy how to come. It's more critical that you only ask your puppy to *come* when *come* is really what you want and you are prepared to reward him. If you want your puppy to get out of the plants, yell, "get outta the plants!" then throw a shake can (a soda can with a few pebbles) at the plants so your puppy thinks you were warning him that the plants were about to explode! Basically, just say what you mean.

Make sure that *come* will mean something really good is about to happen for your puppy. You know the things that are important to your pup. A game of fetch or tug, a treat, a good, vigorous petting session, or a run around the backyard might all be fun for your pup. These are things for you to use as rewards. You want your puppy to think *come* is a signal that the most wonderful thing is about to happen!

Now, say you've taken my advice and your puppy is coming to you reliably and has done so time after time, each time triggering a super fun play or treat session. Say you're in a hurry on a particular day and you decide to tell him to *come*. He comes running as fast as his little legs can carry him, happily expecting his reward of play or treat. Instead, because you're in a hurry, you grab his collar (which can hurt), and throw him in his crate, and leave. In his little doggy brain, he's been punished for coming to you.

At the dog park, he's playing merrily, you decide it's time to go, so you call, "Rover, *come*!" and he runs across the park to come to you. You tell him what a good dog he is, snap the leash on, and go home. In his doggy brain, coming to you ended his fun. There are lots of times when you are calling him to end his fun–when he's digging in the yard...sniffing in the trash...chasing the cat. Those are all FUN for a dog and when you call him away and he comes, make sure you have a party for him. Dance and praise and act like an idiot! Give treats if you have them, otherwise do something else your dog loves. Even let him chase a cat again or go back to digging for a second so you can redirect him to an acceptable digging area. If coming to you always means the end of fun, you can't expect him to *come* very reliably.

Teach your puppy to *come* by using a treat or a toy or another amazing reward. You want to make sure he knows this is BIG fun!

Teaching your puppy to *come* is not hard; it's teaching yourself not to overuse it that's the real trick! Start with a hungry puppy. Have a handful of treats in your left hand. This is very important because timing is important and if you have to go fumbling for a treat in your pocket or a bag or on the counter you will lose valuable momentum. Put one of the treats in your right hand in the tips of your first three fingers and thumb; be ready to replace it quickly. From very near your puppy, reach the hand with the treat toward him. With your puppy looking at you, say your puppy's name followed by *come*! in a happy, excited voice and move the treat toward your knees, luring the puppy to the treat.

When he comes to the treat, GIVE IT! FAST! And then play tug or let him go back to what he was doing. Don't make him sit before giving the treat, because it's the COME we care about. Make a fuss like he just invented the wheel! Big treats, big praise! Just for coming.

If you have help, it's great to have somebody call him from you using the same technique. If you don't have help, just run backward, away from him, calling, "*come*!" Only do this a couple of times, and then release him to play. Keep in mind:

- Always set your puppy up to be successful.
- Always stop when you're ahead.
- Always stop on a positive note.
- Always give your puppy something fun to do after he comes to you; whether it's going back to playing or chewing on a fun bone or playing a game of fetch, make *come* fun!

Practice this all over the place, in the kitchen, in the bathroom, in the yard, on a walk. Go to a "big-box" store and do it in their parking lot or in the garden section. This is a great way to avoid leash pulling, later. Every time you start to lose his attention, call him to you and give a treat.

As your pup starts to associate the word and hand gesture with coming to you, he may start to *come* as you reach your hand out. This will, later, become your hand signal. His response will tell you it's time to start challenging him a little. Make him try a little harder. Start asking him to *come* when there are lots of distractions around. Make it a game. Teach him to *come* to you through and around kids playing ball, skateboarding, and generally being kids. Have him do it past another dog or as you toss his ball past him. It's important to start very close to him. Everybody wants their dog to *come* from a mile away, great! But you have to start close in so you can set him up for success.

BEING ROUGH WITH CHILDREN

The sad truth about puppies and children is that puppies ARE very rough with them and children are completely overmatched. You've spent your child's entire life teaching her to "play nicely" and your puppy has JUST started learning "don't draw blood." Your child will get hurt if you allow the two of them to play together without supervision. On the other hand, some children play too roughly with puppies and need to be supervised so your puppy doesn't get hurt or worse.

Children running past your puppy guarantees your puppy will chase and try to grab. Sure, it's cute in the beginning, but very quickly it's not cute and it becomes dangerous. Sometimes the pup will want to play with the clothing children are wearing. Clothing doesn't feel and it doesn't yelp. When a pup grabs clothing, it pulls away and plays with him. This can be dangerous in the future when your pup grabs clothes and gets flesh instead. It's important to teach your puppy that clothing is part of a person and it gets hurt, too. Use the yelp and stop method described in the section on biting. In any case, children MUST learn not to run, scream, throw their hands in the air, or otherwise incite the puppy to chase and bite. You must always remember that puppies play by chasing and biting. If your child is hurt by your puppy, you are at fault because they should be supervised and under control. But most importantly, no one wants anybody to be hurt. Be vigilant and be fair.

THE MOST IMPORTANT THING IS TO SUPERVISE CHILDREN AND DOGS WHEN THEY PLAY. I KNOW IT DOESN'T SOUND LIKE MUCH FUN, BUT YOUR DOG'S LIFE COULD DEPEND ON IT.

Children need to be taught that they must come up with other ways of playing with dogs. You can have them teach tricks or obedience, have them play a game of fetch or find the toy. You can have the children teach the puppy to play chase with a tug toy as long as the puppy doesn't chase the child. The child can pull the toy on the ground for the puppy to chase it, but if the puppy's mouth touches the child's hand the game must stop. When the puppy learns that he won't get to keep playing he will make sure his teeth stay far away from the child. Chasing bubbles is a game that's fun for kids and puppies, too!

WRESTLING WITH YOUR PUPPY

Wrestling teaches your puppy to play too roughly and, mostly, it teaches him to expect that all humans are ok with it. This can be dangerous to your puppy as he grows into an adult. It's confusing and can lead to aggression.

Dr. Ian Dunbar, internationally recognized as the expert on puppy training, went so far as comparing it to sticking the needle in your dog's vein to give the euthanasia injection. Dogs that are wrestled with get in trouble. Don't wrestle with your pup and don't let anyone else do it either.

LEAVE IT

I have seen pups taught *leave it* in a way that makes them shy and reluctant to work for treats. It's critical that *leave it* be a good thing that is a trick. It needs to be something that earns treats and encourages the puppy to work even more enthusiastically.

Leave it can be used to keep puppies from stealing food from plates, from picking up things from a walk and, eventually, from all kinds of dangers.

Your pup should be hungry when you decide to start *leave it.* Put a toy or a box of tissues (we'll call this a target) on the floor, just out of reach while your puppy watches. As you put it on the ground tell your puppy to *leave it.* Have a treat at the ready and as your puppy starts toward the target, move the treat toward his nose. Say *leave it* again and as his nose swings toward the treat, say, "good!," and give him the treat. Pick up the target and start again.

Within a couple of tries, your puppy should be completely ignoring the target. Then put out two or three more targets of different kinds. Choose things that would normally be very tempting to your puppy. Be prepared! If your pup dodges your hand to get to the targets, put your foot over what he's trying to get and repeat *leave it.* When he looks away from the targets, give a yummy treat!

The puppy should never get the target. Even if you use a treat as a target, the puppy should not get the target. Make sure he sees you pick it up and then give him a treat.

As with all tricks, practice this everywhere and often. Use a plate as a target and then, when your puppy is reliable, put food on the plate. You can add all kinds of variations to this trick. The most important thing to remember is make it fun and set him up for success.

PREVENTING BAD BEHAVIOR FROM BECOMING BAD HABITS

Most bad habits are just annoying; however, dogs that are aggressive over food or possessions are frightening and dangerous. Dogs that dash away from you can be dangerous to themselves! Short of extensive socializing, the following tips are the most critical for your puppy's development.

AGGRESSION IN PUPPIES

Occasionally a puppy will come along with a severe aggression problem. This is not a subtle thing. The puppy will often growl and snarl and bite seriously. The puppy is clearly not playing; he doesn't display any of the play behavior of a normal puppy when he's growling. Some of these puppies will be fine with their owners and some will not. They are usually ok as long as they don't feel pushed. Puppies like this will often "hold a grudge" or not forgive your transgression, whatever it may be.

Some of the puppies are fine at home and your first hint might be when he starts seeing strangers. Or he might be fine with strangers until he gets tired of them.

I have seen 10- and 12-week-old puppies try to stare me down and it made the hair on the back of my neck stand up. These puppies had given their owners only minor worries in the couple of weeks they had been together and the owners are always devastated to hear that they should return the puppy to the breeder. These puppies are more than very likely to be dangerous animals when they grow up. Aggression can be managed, not cured. An aggressive puppy is slightly less than terrifying to me, and I am always fascinated when I meet one. To be honest, I haven't met more than a dozen really scary ones, and even those cause astonishing heartbreak and guilt when the owner returns it to the breeder or shelter.

If you suspect your puppy is aggressive, get a professional opinion right away. A puppy that shows ANY aggression before four months old doesn't need to be living in your home. It will be dangerous and a legal liability. You and all the trainers in the world cannot cure it. You can manage it, but you cannot cure it. The danger will always be there, just under the surface. Love is not enough to make the puppy/dog not bite someone in the face or keep you from losing everything you own if he does. Remember, this book is aimed at the average new dog owner and if you are reading it, you should not have a puppy like this in your home. Even highly experienced, professional trainers will have their work cut out for them with a dog like this and most of them would refuse to take it on. It's not your fault; it's the breeder's. Not intentionally, of course, but the breeder created the problem and it needs NOT to be your problem. The longer you wait the harder it will be to return the pup.

Food Bowl Aggression

It is important to prevent food bowl aggression from ever becoming an issue with your puppy. In the olden days, we were told just to take the bowl away from time to time; just to prove that we could. And if the puppy complained? Well, too bad and if the puppy growled to protect his bowl we were to whack him or knock him down to prove we were the boss!

Well, in our kinder, gentler training environment, it makes sense not to make the food bowl a battleground. The stress of never knowing when your food may be taken away from you is pretty nasty. Some dogs will just fold; others will become progressively more frightened and will anticipate the worst. This can actually CAUSE your puppy to become aggressive around his bowl.

There are the households where Mom and Dad instruct the children to stay away from the puppy while he's eating. Makes sense, right? In this case a perfectly normal puppy grows up thinking that the bowl is his...all his... What happens, then, when one of the kids gets closer to the bowl than normal, or when one of the adults forgets to put the vitamin in the bowl and wants to pick the bowl back up? Well, the puppy and now, the dog, has always had exclusive access to the bowl and is resentful that someone is horning in on his meal. He growls, you freeze in surprise. Was that really YOUR dog growling at you? Your dog sees you freeze and realizes that the growl had impact; by the time you gather your thoughts, he has too. You reach again for the bowl, and this time the growl is accompanied by bared teeth. You are in shock and yell, "hey!" and your dog realizes that you really are fighting him for the food. He escalates and so do you. Now you're in trouble.

There's pretty much no turning back at this point. Both you and your dog are feeling threatened and scared and righteous. Bad gets worse until you wonder if you will have to have your pal euthanized because of this.

FOOD BOWL EXERCISES

Food bowl aggression is much easier to prevent than cure. Each time you feed your puppy, have a few pieces of something special in your hand. Put the food bowl on the floor and then reach in to it. Swirl your hand around as if you're looking for something, then pull your hand out and show your pup the yummy treat you "found" in his bowl! It's magic! He's pretty sure that wasn't in there when you first put the bowl down! How you found something delicious in there is a happy mystery. "Do it again! Do it again!" he cries. So do him a favor and do it again! Everyone in your family should show your puppy that they, too, can perform this magic trick! If there is no one else in your family, invite people over to do the trick. This is such an important thing, you really can't afford not to take the time to do it. You want your puppy not just to tolerate people reaching into his food bowl, but to crave it!

After a few days of the magic trick, start picking his bowl back up after you put it down. Put the bowl back on the counter and put in a scoop of canned food or low fat cottage cheese or yogurt, then give it back. Your puppy will be so happy to have you take his bowl!

If your puppy is already too aggressive to let you reach into his bowl, get rid of the bowl. Start feeding him by hand, one piece at a time. Then, after a week or two, reintroduce the bowl. Just put it on the floor, near where you have been hand feeding him. Every day move it closer to where you want to feed him 'til after several days you can start dropping the pieces of kibble into the bowl. Try the "magic trick" at this point. Reach into the bowl and pull out a treat and give it to him. Drop kibble 10 or 15 times, then reach in and pull out a treat again. At this point if your puppy threatens you at all, you need a trainer immediately. DO NOT put yourself or your family in danger, as a dog that becomes aggressive over food after this amount of training will be dangerous to you.

STEALING

Our adorable puppies are always into things! They are exploring their world with their mouths and they pick things up because they can. Sometimes your pup may pick something up that you don't want him to have.

If you have something you don't want destroyed, keep it away from your puppy. If your puppy chews on things (and all puppies do) it's your responsibility to keep him safe. You have to keep things away from him that could hurt him. It doesn't work to wait 'til he has something, then take it away and scold him. The more fuss you make about getting an object away from him, the more valuable he thinks it is and the more he'll steal it and use it to get you to interact with him. How many times have you chased him around the coffee table trying to get him to give back the sock? You may have been furious but your dog was having a blast! What a fun game!

PICK YOUR BATTLES! Leaves in the backyard? Let the puppy chew on them. Snails? Worms? Sticks? IGNORE! Rocks? Redirect your puppy's attention by tossing a treat or a toy past the rock. Don't overreact! Puppies have lived in backyards for thousands of years without needing people to tackle them and dig grass out of their mouths. Think about this, we are the humans. We have ALL of the coolest stuff in the world! We have access to the cookies, the food, the can opener, we can open doors and unwrap chewies. When we want something they have, they think it must be more exciting than they thought! It's TREASURE! So, not only will they try to keep it, but they are FAR more likely to start looking for more of it and then SWALLOWING it before you can steal it. In Dog Law, an adult would never forcibly take something from a puppy; it just isn't done. When we do it, it attaches an incredible emotional element and can facilitate a future obsession.

A better option, if it's something you don't want him to damage, is to go to the kitchen and get a treat. Show him you have the treat and ask him if he wants to trade. Or go get one of his favorite toys, sit on the floor with your back to him, and start playing merrily. He won't be able to resist and will come to see what you're doing or what you have to eat. Smile and greet him. DON'T REACH FOR HIM OR WHAT HE HAS; that will just teach him never to fall for that trick again. When he's interested in the game you're playing or the treat, engage him in play or with a lure and work your way to his crate or a room you can confine him in for a few minutes. THEN go back and pick up whatever it was that he had. This keeps him from learning that he can tease you and make you chase him by finding things that you value.

The most important thing is prevention. Keep him from learning to pick up your things. You can also use *leave it,* but *trade* works really well. You just have to make sure you don't wait until he's got something he shouldn't to teach it.

TRADE

Teach *trade* by walking up to your puppy when he's chewing on a chewie or playing with a toy. Have a special treat in your hand (no Milk Bones! Something smelly and chewy and wonderful). And say, "hey Rover, wanna trade?" Then offer the treat. Most puppies will happily leave what they have for the treat. Take his toy or chewie and quickly give it back. Let him go back to his toy and then do it again. And again and again. Then toss a treat away from him, when he goes to get it, take his toy, examine it thoroughly, smiling and telling him what a cool toy it is, then give him a treat and give the toy back. This will need to be practiced with progressively more exciting toys and treasures until he is bringing them to you to show them off!

Remember that, in his mind, if you want it, it must be VERY special.

COLLAR GRABS

Teach your puppy to enjoy being grabbed by the collar. Too many dogs dash out of reach when someone reaches for their collar. This may prevent them from being saved by a Good Samaritan in the case of an emergency. Some dogs actually panic if their collar is held by a stranger, and may bite! Often, the only time we grab a dog by its collar is when it's in trouble. I can always tell a puppy that's been grabbed by the collar when it comes. He comes to the owner, and then hovers just out of reach. This often drives the owner NUTS! Which then makes the owner angry, which then makes the puppy POSITIVE that he made the right decision by keeping his distance! So, the bottom line is teaching him that being grabbed by the collar means wonderful things are soon to follow.

Have treats in your pocket as you're walking through the house, going about your business. Walk past your puppy, grab his collar, stuff treats into his mouth, tell him what a good dog he is, release his collar, and continue on your way. Next time you go past him, repeat it. Don't give a command or tell him to do anything. Just cruise by and grab. The treats should be pretty yummy because collar grabs are scary for some pups. Have everyone in the family and all of your guests do the same thing. Soon your pup should be looking hopefully at you whenever you walk by.

When your pup is good at this, lead him by the collar to a sofa or chair, sit down, and continue to give treats. Give the treats one at a time and praise like mad when he lets you lead him by the collar. Leading by the collar is also very scary for many puppies so be generous with treats and praise and make sure to reassure him.

PREVENTING SEPARATION ANXIETY

Separation anxiety can be a very serious, even life-threatening, problem for dogs. It has a pretty specific definition, but generally refers to a dog that is terrified to be left alone. These dogs commonly cry, whine, howl, urinate, defecate, drool, vomit, claw at doors, chew doorframes, and chew or force their way out of crates and kennels. Some of them chew through walls and fences and may jump through windows. Beyond the difficulty of managing a dog like this, imagine their level of terror. What a horrible life to live.

Prevention is the key. Little tiny things we do in our day-to-day activities can cause a little anxiety to grow until it's uncontrollable. Following are some recommendations to keep your puppy from developing separation anxiety as an adult.

As flattering as it is, when your puppy is screaming and crying in excitement because you've been gone all day, the worst thing you can do is scoop him up and cuddle and kiss and reassure him. This convinces him that it really WAS a big deal that you were gone and that you were nervous about it, too. Even though your human heart flutters when you see him like that, the best thing to do is stay calm and matter-of-fact. Smile, let him out of his confinement area, and take him straight outside to go potty. Once he's gone potty, you can make a big fuss over him, because then it's about his potty, not you being gone.

When you leave your puppy (and you should!), you can give as big a goodbye as you like, as long as you stop at least 20 minutes before you leave. That's right. NO GOODBYES within 20 minutes of you leaving. Well, ok, you can SAY one quick, casual "goodbye," but that's it! Long, sad, drawn out goodbyes scare puppies. They wonder why on earth you would leave them if it's so scary! When you're gone, they pretty much forget about you and go to sleep. They may wake up and call you, but when you don't come, they find something to do. Chewing on their bone, working food out of their kong, wrestling with their knotted, safe rope are all things that will keep them busy until it's time for their next nap (30-40 minutes or so). Of course, when you get home they'll be happy to see you; but if you run to them and snatch them up and "buy into" their hysteria, you will eventually convince them that they should be afraid. You will make their hysteria stronger and longer lasting until they turn into maniacs.

The more dramatic your comings and goings, the harder it is for your puppy to understand that it's ok for you to go. Practice leaving often, when you're not really leaving. Pick up your keys, put on your jacket, put your pup in his confinement area (crate), and then reverse it all! Do that over and over to desensitize you and your puppy to your leaving.

Another thing that can really lead to separation anxiety is your puppy following you from room to room through the day. Again, while flattering, it's not good for him! First, he needs to sleep and if he follows you everywhere, it's hard for him to relax and really sleep. Frequently, puppies will follow their owners, and then plop down from exhaustion and fall asleep again, only to wake when you move again and repeat the whole process. This is really hard on a puppy.

Put him in his crate while you're home sometimes. I usually recommend two to four hours a day while you're home. It doesn't need to be all in one stretch, an hour here, an hour there. Good times to crate him are during the morning hours while you're getting everybody ready to go to work and school; dinnertime when he shouldn't be under your feet while you're cooking anyway; and in the evening while you're watching your favorite show. It's VERY important for him to learn to comfort himself while you're home. The more he follows you, the more likely he will suffer from separation anxiety. Put the crate in the busiest part of the house, so he can see everything going on. Make him a part of the household, but without the chaos that usually accompanies a puppy at those times of day.

Protect your puppy! Always act like there's nothing to be afraid of. You and I KNOW, beyond a doubt, that he really doesn't need to fear anything while you're gone. LET HIM IN ON THE SECRET! You may save his life.

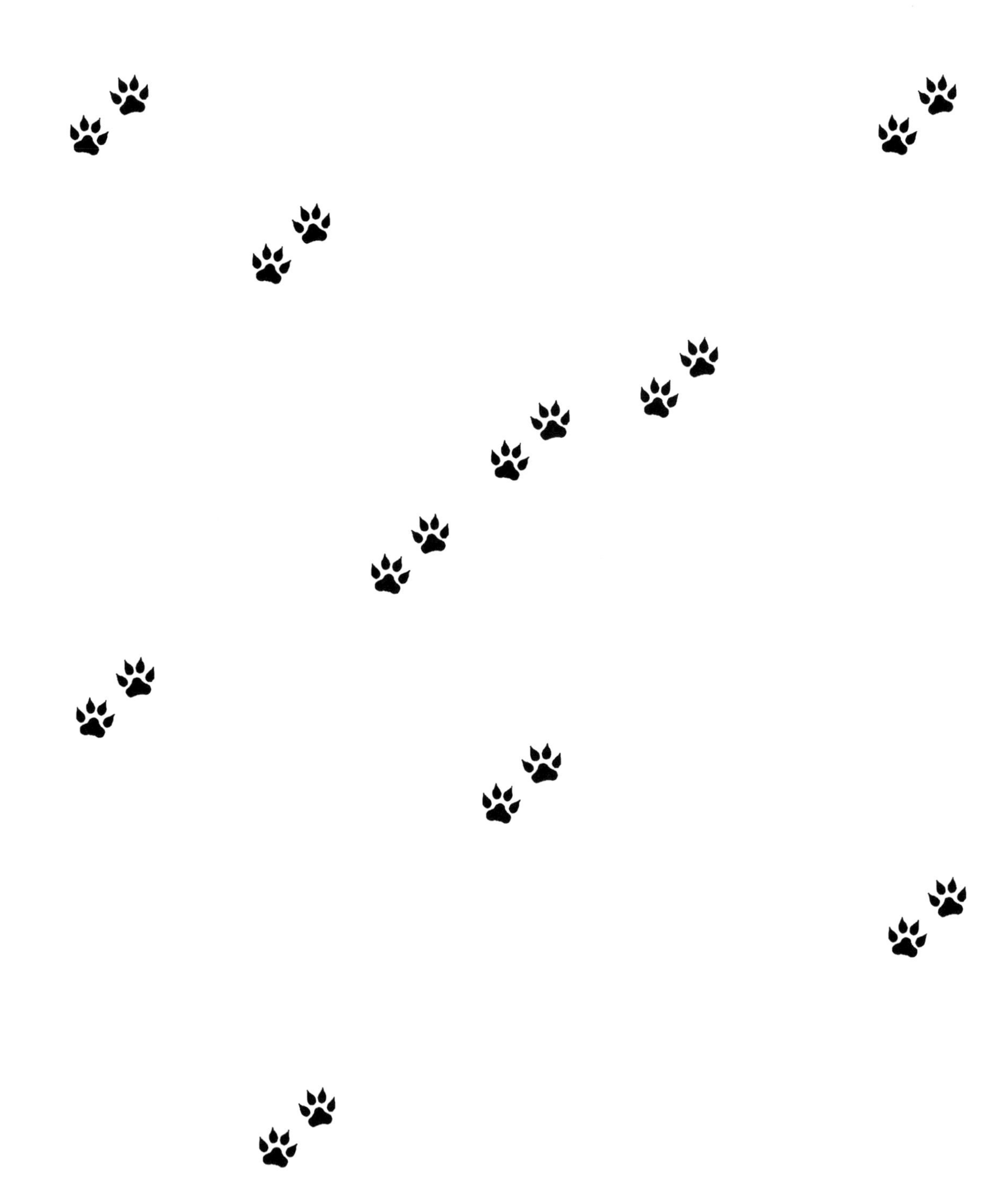

REWARDS

Most humans think of rewards for dogs as either a pat on the head or food. None of us wants to have to carry around treats forever; it feels like we have to bribe our best friend to like us! Dogs aren't people (thank goodness!!), which has a lot to do with why we love them. They respond to things differently than we do. They are really excited about certain things in their lives, and these things work well to motivate them to work for us. I know, I know, they should do it because they love us! They love us almost NO MATTER what we do or don't do for them but work is work and most dogs don't really have the attachment to their chores that we have. They don't care where they go potty, we do. They don't care where they walk, we do. Stay? Stay? Oh, c'mon! That's soooo human! They're dogs! Those are all human issues. But we want them to care, and to get to that level, we need to train them.

TWO WAYS TO TRAIN A DOG

There are lots of variations on both, but two basic methods. One is the "traditional" way. This is the way most people are familiar with. This entails using "corrections" and praise. The dog learns that by avoiding corrections, he earns praise. The problem with this method is that the corrections are painful and can damage your relationship with your dog. Lots of people mistake this as a dog that is doing it because "he loves me." Yes, he does love you, but he's doing it because if he doesn't, you'll hurt him by "correcting" him.

For instance, to teach *sit* the traditional way, you pull up hard on the dog's collar (most traditional trainers recommend a choke chain) and push down on your dog's butt. When the dog tries to move away, you push and pull harder. The dog tries to move away because he's scared. His neck is being pulled straight up and someone is trying to knock him down! His breathing is impaired because of where the collar is, and his instinct is to give in to the pressure of the collar to make it stop. But because you are pushing down on his butt at the same time he thinks he might not be able to breathe any more. He doesn't know the pressure will stop if he sits. So he struggles to make you stop choking him and, eventually, you get his butt on the ground and tell him "Good Dog." He jumps back up because he's free and he can breathe. So you have to make him sit again and you can't figure out why he doesn't get it and why he keeps making you do this to him. He doesn't get it because he is confused about why you would be attacking him for no reason. You haven't given him a chance to learn it before you "punish" him for not doing it.

I used so-called traditional methods for decades. They work and they work well. I considered it "tough love."

And then a little disabled dog came into my life. She had a neck injury as a puppy and had many severe medical problems. She spent her first few months in constant pain and had lots of "issues." I suddenly realized that I was completely unequipped to train a dog I didn't want to hurt or scare.

As I researched training methods, I realized that if *this* puppy shouldn't be yanked on and scared, confused and hurt as an acceptable part of her training then why should any other puppy or dog?

It was an ugly and scary reality. I couldn't train a dog without hurting it.

So I learned about "luring" and positive reinforcement, which is really just demonstrating what you want your dog to do by using a treat or something motivating, then when he does what you asked for, act like he just invented the wheel! When he doesn't do it right, take away the opportunity to earn a reward. Give him another demonstration, if he needs it, and then offer the chance to win again.

Food works. Period. We have a choice in dog training and the choice is pretty cut and dried. Train with pain or train with food. I've done it the pain way, and believe me, the food way is better. This doesn't mean you'll never yell at your dog or that your dog will never have his neck yanked; dogs do really dopey things sometimes. People do, too.

But why not take advantage of your dog's desire to eat everything in your hand? Why not control your dog through the science of learning theory as opposed to the violence of leftover WWII training methods?

I recently had a newly adopted Golden Retriever come to class with his new family. He was about 80 pounds of HAPPY! Bouncy and crazy. When his family came the next week, the little girl (maybe four years old?), in her tiny, sweet, little voice, said, "Rex, come!" and Rex came flying over to her, where he promptly sat and laid down upon her tiny commands. I turned to the class and said, "Do you think she could have made Rex do that with a choke chain or pinch collar?" If you think that food is wimpy, think about the little girl who out powered her 80 pound dog because she had what he wanted. He who has the food controls the world, in a dog's mind.

HOW TO USE REWARDS

Rewards are better when they're unpredictable. For a Retriever the best reward might be a quick game of fetch. For a Poodle the best reward might be for you to sit on the ground and cuddle for a minute. For a dog park fiend, a reward might be a trip to the dog park, and for a Basset Hound, it might be five minutes of uninterrupted sniffing in a really exciting bush! But for nearly all of them, treats work wonderfully for helping them understand why they should learn something as useless (to them) and boring as *stay*. Treats are easy to have available, they can be eaten quickly so you can go back to work quickly and dogs LOVE 'em! Later, start adding in the really good stuff like tummy rubs on the couch and rides in the car.

Instead of my dogs working to avoid punishment, they work to engage me, they work to make me give them a treat, and they work because at some point, they will get a special moment with me. "They work because they love me!" Being with me means good things are likely to happen. I didn't think it was possible, but they do work to please me. Pleasing me makes me happy, and when Mom's happy, everyone's happy.

As you can see, rewards are anything your dog wants: outside, inside, dinner, treats, chase the squirrel, or ride in the car. The list could go on forever. Rewards can even be getting away from something undesirable, like a tight leash. The reward for walking next to you is eventually a loose leash. But in the beginning, it includes treats, praise, crazy play, and going for a walk. Tiny kibble works great for around the house, but you'll need something special for really stressful or distracting areas. They should make your dog crazy for them! I joke that even a super stubborn dog would learn to drive a car for the right kind of treat! I call these "driving lesson" treats and they should be smelly and easy to eat quickly. It's best if they are easy to handle, somewhat dry, not greasy, and don't melt in your hand. You get more mileage from soft or semi-soft treats like Bil Jac liver treats, pepperoni, or other grocery store treats.

You can make wonderful treats from chicken hot dogs by microwaving them. Cut them into tiny bits and microwave on a paper plate for 2 minutes at a time. Blot with a paper towel to absorb any grease between each cooking cycle. Do this several times during the cooking process. When the pieces are becoming dark and smelling strong, let them cool for several minutes. They should become crunchy, like a cracker. They will keep, unrefrigerated, for several days. They are easy to handle and NOT greasy and most dogs go nuts for them.

I usually recommend an assortment of treats. Some good, some better, some incredible! Switch from time to time. If you got the exact same tee shirt every time you

parked perfectly, you'd be dyin' to figure out how to get the coffee mug! Even if you didn't really care for coffee mugs! It's something new and different and you just might like it. It comes back to that intermittent reward concept. He may get treats and treats are great but he may get an AMAZING treat!

PUNISHMENT

Punishment is anything that keeps your dog from getting a reward. So if you are about to let your dog outside and you ask him to *sit* and he doesn't, you let go of the doorknob and go to another room. Your dog will be frustrated and will try to figure out what happened. It may take several aborted attempts, but he will finally "get" that he needs to sit, even when your hand is on the doorknob!

If he's being a dimwit when you're about to feed him, dancing around and being rude, put his bowl on the counter and go back to what you were doing. Give him five minutes to stew about why he didn't get fed, then try again. You shouldn't have to say anything to him to cue him to be calm. If he acts calm, get ready to give him his bowl, if he gets crazy, put it back. When you put the bowl back you can use a "too bad" or "nope" and walk away. He will figure out, quickly, that he blew it. Then he will try to figure out what you want. Most dogs' "default" is sit. When he sits (without you having told him to) he gets his dinner. Unless he pops up as you start to put it down...timing is everything. His butt must remain on the ground to get his reward.

Punishment might be a time out. Or it might be pulling the car over and stopping it, if he's acting like a maniac while you're driving. If he pulls you to the dog park, punishment might be going the opposite direction for a few steps or just stopping and not letting him get any closer until he pays attention to you. Punishment doesn't have to be violent or loud or physically painful. It just has to communicate that he made a bad decision. This helps him have a little control over his life; it gives him tools to get what he wants without making you mad. If it's something big, you can scold him. Dogs don't need to be scared or hurt to learn what we want.

TIMING

Timing is everything. Make sure you reward or punish the behavior you actually want. I see many people teach their dogs, "sit-until-I-start-to-bend-over-to-give-you-your-reward-then-stand-up-and-take-it-from-my-hand." These are the people who don't understand why their dog can't do a *sit-stay*. The dog can't do a *sit-stay* because it has been taught that *sit* means sit, then stand!

Be very aware of what your dog is doing when he actually GETS the reward or punishment; is that really what you intended? Really focus and if it's going too fast for you, slow the whole thing down by slowing all of your motions and words. You may just have to STOP what you're doing and regroup. If your dog consistently pops up from a *down* right before you give him a treat, it's because you've inadvertently taught him to. Start re-teaching it the way you want it. Say, "Too bad" in a sweet tone of voice and give him lots of "you're getting warmer" cues to keep him working happily.

THE EARLY STAGES OF TRAINING

The early stages of training are pretty treat-dense. Treats are a predictable and easy way to keep your dog's attention and demonstrate new moves and tricks. Always have

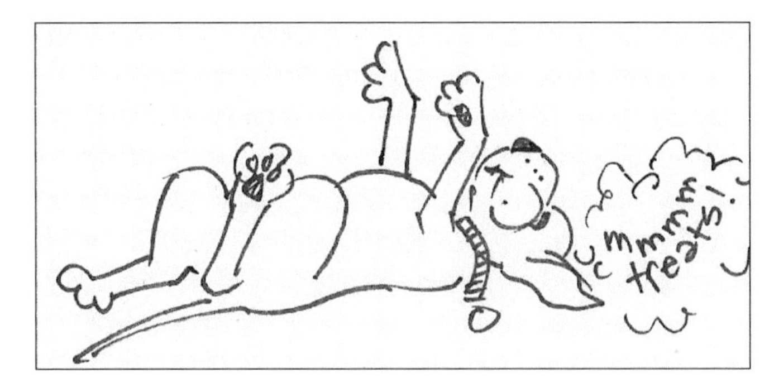

treats ready. This means in your hand, ready to dispense. NOT in a pocket or baggie or treat bag. It's ok to have a backup supply in those places, but you need ALWAYS to have several at the ready, in your hand. I try to lure with my right hand and initially will give that treat to the dog. As the dog starts to "get it," I'll continue luring (this will become a hand signal very quickly) with my right hand, but the hand will be empty. I give the treat with my left. This changes the dog's focus from following the treat to understanding the hand signal. It can take away the complaint of dogs not doing something unless you show them a treat. *Make sure you make this change after no more than 12 repetitions.*

If I see a dog really working to do something, really struggling to focus, and ignoring distractions, I always want to show my appreciation with an extra special reward. Whether it is food or a game, you want to make sure it makes an impression and that he'll remember it next time he has to decide, "Go to dad? Or chase the squirrel?" Also, if he gives me a spectacular performance, a perfect *sit,* or a super quick *down,* I will make sure I give an especially appreciative reward, to increase the chances of that performance repeating.

AS HE LEARNS

As he learns how the tricks work and how to perform them, start spacing the rewards farther and farther apart. This doesn't mean that after doing the trick three times you can stop giving treats! If you just stop giving them or you stop too quickly and don't replace them with a different reward, you may cause the dog to stop doing them altogether. Have you ever put money in a soda machine and not gotten a soda? It will be a while before you try that machine again. The same thing goes for your dog and you withholding treats. It's important to teach him that just because you have treats it doesn't mean he's going to get them. He will want to work harder to do it right and get a reward. Doing anything without frequent and exciting rewards will take some time. Don't be stingy with rewards; be generous and SMART.

"Fading" the treats is as important as using treats. If you use treats and don't fade them, you get the dog who "won't do anything if I don't have treats in my hand". All of the instructions, below, will coach you on your hand signals; you'll be using your right hand to lure the puppy through the trick then giving him the reward from the same hand. But, when your puppy has shown that he understands the concept of a new trick, hopefully within 3 repetitions, move the treat from your right hand to your left. Continue to give the hand signal as if you have a treat in it, but now the actual treat is coming from your left. Within a few more repetitions, move the treats to your left pocket and take treats out of your pocket for each successful effort. Then move the treats to the kitchen counter and when your puppy performs for you say, in the living room, run with him to the kitchen for a treat! Taking these important steps will assure that your puppy never says, "Nope", just because you don't' have a treat.

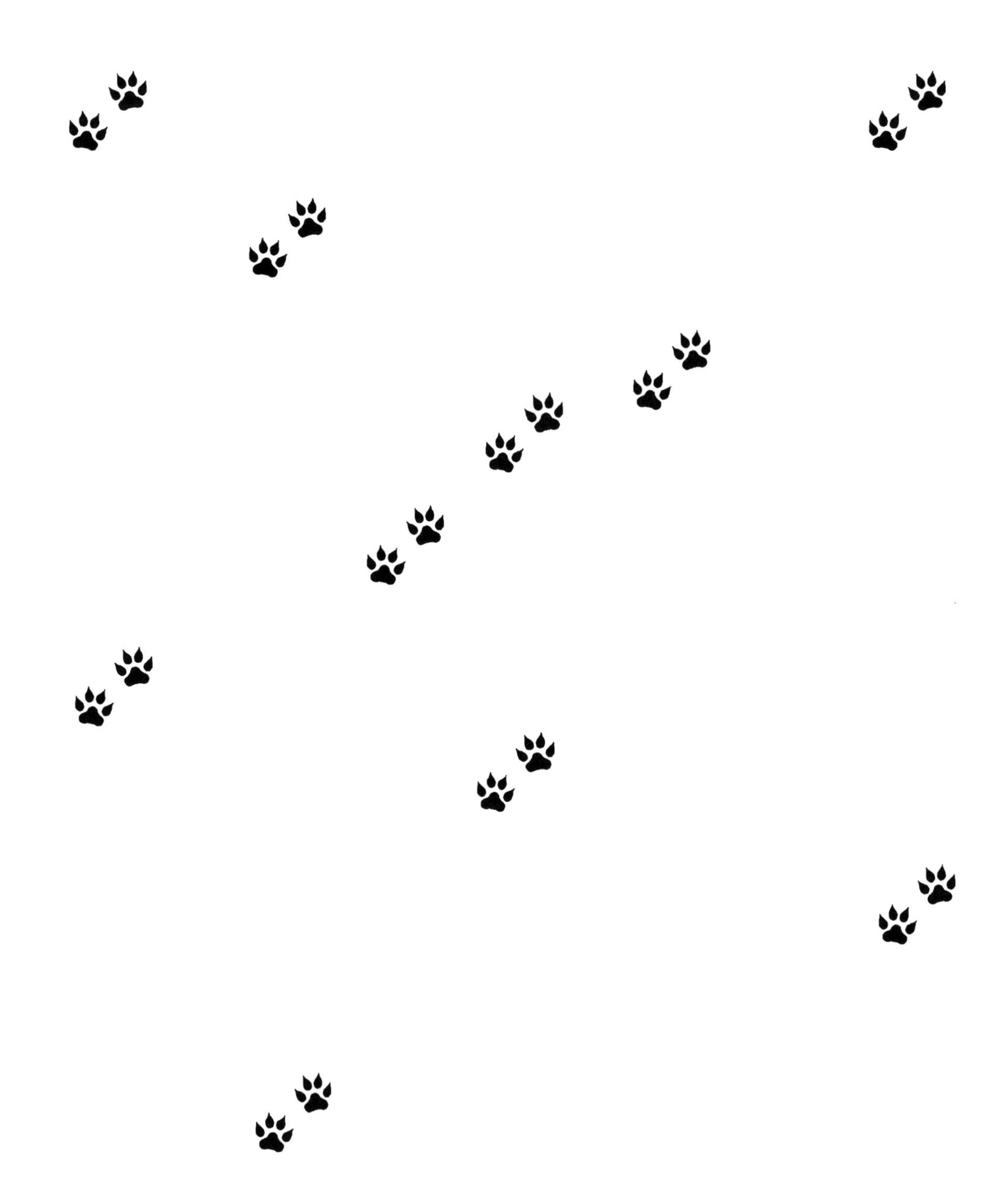

LOOSE LEASH WALKING

Loose leash walking is the second most requested training I provide. It's something that everybody thinks they should have but most seem not to be able to achieve. I believe that the single reason for failure is the leash! Now, now...I know. You have to have a leash! How will you keep your dog from running away, without a leash!

THE LEASH AS RESTRAINT

Imagine not having a leash. How would you control your dog if you didn't have a leash? Would you speak differently? Would you act differently? From the time you brought your adorable puppy or rambunctious shelter dog home, what have you been doing with your leash? Pulling on it! You pull to make him follow you, you pull to make him come to you, you pull to keep his attention, and you pull to keep him away from things. How would you have accomplished these things without a leash? Would you have? If you didn't have a leash, you would have to pay very close attention to your dog. You would be very clear with your communication with him and you would have to come up with a way to make him want to stay with you. Hmmmmm... You thought you were already doing that, didn't you?

We rely way too much on leashes to position our dogs, to control our dogs, and to restrain our dogs. Restraining is not training. I'm not saying lose the leash, but we need to work on pretending it's not there.

Most people come to my classes with a flat buckle collar and an assortment of ez grip leashes. The leashes have had knots tied in them to prevent the dog from dragging it through the hands, they have extra handles so you can really dig your heels in and hold your dog back from anything he thinks might be fun, and they're super-duper thick so you won't break them by pulling your dog back. Leashes should be like a safety net; they're in case something goes wrong. Instead, they have become our main means of control/communication with our dogs. Without a leash, most of us are lost.

THE PEOPLE PROBLEM

I can't tell you how often I hear, "My dog pulls constantly, I can't take her anywhere!" When I convince the person to stop pulling on the leash, the dog stops pulling, too. Very often the dog pulls because we've trained it to. Put your dog's leash on and go stand in the front yard. Set a timer for five minutes. Just stand in the front yard. No walking, no commands. Give your dog the entire length of its leash. Just hold the end of the leash. Ok, five minutes are up. How long is your leash? My bet is that it's wrapped around your hand at least a few times but you're probably holding it so your dog has less than half the actual length of the leash. Why is this bad? Because even if the dog loosens the leash, we keep taking up the slack, making it tight again. How can a dog learn to keep the leash loose when we can't?

So, you ask, "What can I do? My dog has to have a leash on, how do I make him stop pulling?" Well, the first thing you have to do is read the chapter on rewards. It will explain a lot about how dogs learn and think and it will make the instructions here make more sense. Next, you have to make a commitment to yourself and your dog not to pull on his neck unless he's being a twerp or he's in danger. Yes, a leash is an absolute MUST. But using it kindly is at least as important.

I mentioned earlier that we've trained our dogs to pull on the leash. We have. We have taught them that to get what they want they have to pull, and the harder they pull the more likely they are to get what they really want. You're probably thinking that's not you,

you've tried hard to make your dog walk next to you. The training I'm talking about is inadvertent. It happens accidentally. It started the first couple of times your dog was on a leash. Remember reading about an and how well it works? Each time your dog successfully gets where he wants to go while he's pulling, the more convinced he is that's what you want.

ATTENTION

So, how to get our dogs somewhere without them pulling? The most important thing to remember is, "Loose leash, Loose leash, Loose leash." If your leash is loose you have to rely on something else to keep your dog close to you. You will be relying on rewards consisting of treats and other things your dog loves (including that bush he always has to sniff because there was a cat in it once), animation, communication, and attention. You will need to completely engage your dog's attention and act like he just invented the wheel when he gets it right. If your neighbors aren't pointing out the window saying, "Charlie! Come quick! That crazy neighbor is walking her dog again!" you're not praising animatedly enough.

It's just as important for you to pay attention to your dog: where he is, what he's doing, who he's bothering. Your dog should not be allowed to go and stick his face where it's not welcome. And you should assume that it's not welcome anywhere. Your dog should be your focus whenever he's on leash.

COLLARS AND LEASHES

No collar should ever be tightened for more than an instant. Use words, gestures, distraction, or just go the other way to get your dog's attention back on you. If your dog is looking at you, his leash should be loose and you should be looking at him, praising like mad.

KNOW WHAT YOU WANT

On to the "how to." You have to think of loose leash walking as the only kind of walking that you will ever accept. It is critically important that your dog understand there is only one set of rules. I have seen dogs with advanced obedience titles dragging their owners around show grounds or around town. I have seen dogs with no formal training walking politely, on a loose leash, through the most distracting scenes you can imagine. The point is that dogs will learn that you only expect them to walk politely at class or on a certain walk or for the first five minutes of the walk. They learn this by testing your rules. They're not being bad or devious; they just need to know they have it right, so they test. "Do you want it here? Ok, how about here? Ok, how about when you're talking to your friend? How about when you're on the phone? On the way into the dog park? REALLY? You never said that before! How about now? Now? Here? Even if I __________? Oh, here comes a big scary dog! NOW?!!! You MUST be kidding!"

So you have to know what you want and set your dog up for success, which means no going for long walks until your dog "gets it." You have to make sure that you can and will pay attention to your dog during the entire walk and that you can help him get it right. Some people find that it's easier to drive their dog somewhere he's not used to being. This can help eliminate the "habit" part of the equation. To change a habit in an adult dog takes from 8-12 weeks of serious work. Sometimes it's easier to teach your dog what you want in a different environment, and then transfer it to the physical area that triggers the old, undesirable behavior. Treat each walk as a training session. No going for walks unless you're willing to treat it as a training session...at least 'til you both understand the intricacies.

Lastly, most importantly, you need to learn to recognize where you want your dog. This is loose leash walking, not *heel,* and you need to have a picture in your mind of what you will and won't accept from your dog. I don't mind my dogs being in front of me a little. They can drift off to the side and sniff a little or lag behind a tiny bit. Even when they're in front of me, their ears constantly cock back to me and they will physically turn and look when I move quickly. I can verbally ask them to come in closer to me by saying *heel* and they return to my side. This is not a show-ring *heel,* but it's what I want from my dogs. I use *heel* to keep my dogs next to me in a crowded, super stimulating, or dangerous environment.

We have to remember that, for a dog, *heel* is not fun. It's work. When we take our dogs for walks, most of us are doing it for enjoyment. Enjoyment for your dog is seeing the sights, smelling the smells, and watching for excitement. These things are hard to do if you are demanding that he perform a classic *heel* through the whole walk. *Heel* requires that his right shoulder be in line with your left knee. That's tough positioning. That's hard work for both of you and, above all, it's boring!! But walking should be a pleasure for both of you and you should be in charge.

I recommend that you imagine a "comfort zone" around you. That's the area that will make both you and your dog comfortable, he'll be comfortable because he can keep track of you and you'll be comfortable because he's happy and not pulling on the leash. A circle three to four feet around you usually works well. Now, your job is to make sure you make that area comfortable for him by not pulling on him and yanking him when he's in it. His job is to make you comfortable by not pulling or yanking on you! Sounds great, doesn't it?

TECHNIQUES

There are a couple of techniques to master. One is giving your dog the entire length of his leash to work with. I recommend nothing shorter than a six-foot leash and absolutely no retractable leads! Get the lightest weight leash you can safely use. I've NEVER seen a dog that needed a double layered, triple stitched, heavy duty, five-pound leash. Chain leashes are a no-no because they are hard on your hands; which makes it less likely that you'll use it correctly. Hold the leash in your left hand. Just the handle. No more. Don't gather it up and don't wrap it around your hand over and over to "get a better grip." This is probably the hardest part for people to learn and it really helps to have somebody watch you in the beginning. Have your spotter tell you when you gather the leash or wrap the leash or raise your hand in the air to take up slack. You won't know you're doing it, I almost guarantee. Most people cannot keep slack in the leash. If your dog gets tangled in the leash, he will learn to untangle himself. He may trip on it once or twice, but it's because HE'S NEVER HAD SLACK IN HIS LEASH BEFORE AND HE DOESN'T RECOGNIZE IT! He WILL learn to untangle himself.

The next thing to master is the right about turn. This turn should be made as if you're late to an appointment and you just realized you forgot your keys. It should be a PIVOT on the ball of your left foot and then walk quickly in the opposite direction. Practice this without your dog a few times. Walk out quickly and assertively. Pick something in front of you to walk toward and go. Really go. Then think, turn! Quickly PIVOT on your left foot, pushing off hard. What we're after is a sharp, quick turn; not a "take a couple of steps and end up going the opposite direction." You should end up walking back in *exactly* the path you made on your way out. This is easier if you practice on the lines in a tennis court or parking lot lines.

STARTING OUT

Once you're comfortable with the concepts mentioned above, it's time to explain the deal to your dog. Start with making him wait quietly and calmly to have his leash clipped on. If he bombs around making you struggle or does anything besides wait quietly, the leash goes back where it was and you go sit down. Try again in a couple of minutes. Don't say, "sit" or "stay." Don't say anything until you decide to put the leash down. Then just say, "nope" in a "too bad" tone of voice. Nothing else. You want him to learn that to get what he wants (a walk) he must be calm and quiet. This spills over into all other aspects of his relationship with you, especially walking. Most dogs learn very quickly (five to eight tries) not to act like a wild thing, without any "command" from you. This is what we're after. You want him to *be* calm and quiet, not just when you tell him to be.

Once your dog is leashed, he needs to learn not to charge out the door. Dogs have different tolerances of excitement. Some dogs lose it as you're reaching for the doorknob, others don't get excited at all. If your dog becomes overexcited and stops being polite, you need to let him know he's wrong. If he blows it as you open the door, close the door. Hard and loud. NOT ON HIM. But definitely to startle him. Do it again and again as he starts to push through the door without you. As before, five to eight tries will convince him that he needs to see what you're thinking. He will, most likely, back up and look at you. He may even sit! Again, this is with no verbal reminders. When he looks at you, instead of the door, smile and go to open the door again. Be prepared for him to try to dash through it one more time. Close the door in his face. "AHA! I get it!" And he will.

This is the theme of training. Your dog gets what he wants by looking at you, being calm and quiet, and waiting for you to let him know when it's ok to do whatever is next.

So, as you go out the door and your dog flies down the walkway (he's not paying attention to you if he's dashing past you), do your "I forgot my keys" turn and call, call, call your puppy and head back into the house, dragging him along behind if need be. Then start out the door again using the door to remind him of the manners he just learned. He just needs to know you mean it. Don't get angry, don't get discouraged. It will work. Stay happy and matter-of-fact. If you start to become less than happy, ask your dog to sit or something easy and then quit. Go play fetch or something physical to help both of you blow off some steam and laugh (yes, dogs laugh). Then, try again later.

KEEP IT FUN

Then you can treat it almost like a game of keep away. You are keeping him from catching you, and in the process, you become a reward! Dogs love to chase; use that love to get a quick and happy, loose leash walking dog. Run three steps forward, then four steps to the side the a few steps forward again. Talk to him the whole time. Encourage him to keep himself in his comfort zone. Make it fun! You'll see your dog trying and you'll see his tail come up and his mouth open in happiness. Stop fast and ask him to sit! Then tease him...start to lean forward, ask him if he's ready. "Ready? Ready?? Are you ready? Let's go!!" and then run forward again. Stop suddenly and praise like the dickens when he stops with you. Tease him again. Don't let him start forward until you do. Then take off running again. Stop quickly. Repeat this a couple of times and then give him a release word (anything but "ok") to let him know it is ok to take a break. Let him drift and sniff around and relax, but don't let him pull. When he starts pulling on the leash do a turn and walk away. He will learn to keep an eye on you all the time.

Always remember why your dog likes to go for walks and what he's willing to suffer to do it. Leash pulling isn't comfortable for him either but he thinks that's what it takes to go for a walk, so he'll put up with it. Always remember to set your dog up for success. He can't learn the right way to do it if he never gets the chance to do it right. Start with small

steps. Be consistent with your rules. Don't let him pull if you don't want him to pull. Remember to let him know when he's right. If you don't tell him he's right, he won't know!

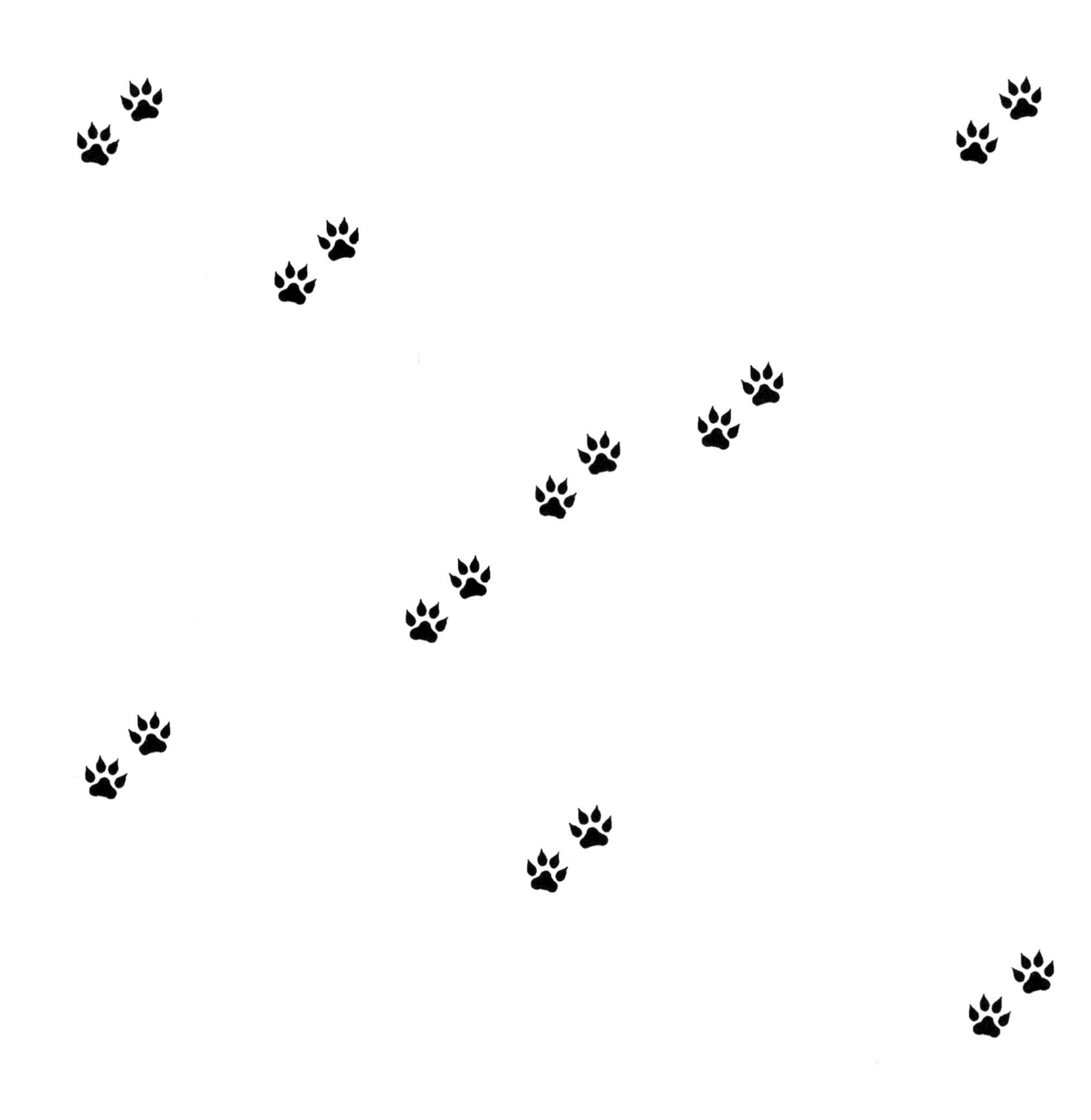

TRICKS

Tricks are not just for kids! Tricks are simply off-leash obedience, taught in a fun and happy way. Remember this part...tricks are off-leash obedience! Think about it, have you ever seen dogs being forced through tricks on a leash? Some of the tricks you will recognize as "obedience commands." I much prefer that people teach their dogs these "commands" as tricks. Tricks are fun and our faces look different when we're having fun than when we're teaching commands. Dogs CARE what our faces look like! They want us to look happy and friendly. When we teach "commands," our faces end up looking like we're drill sergeants and our dogs wonder what's wrong. It can make them want to avoid training sessions. Teaching tricks, on the other hand, makes us more relaxed, makes us laugh, and makes our dogs enjoy it!

BUILDING A BRIDGE

You won't always be able to give your dog a reward right away. He may be far from you doing something good or he may be doing something good while you just can't give him a reward. You won't always WANT to give your dog a reward right then and there and you will sometimes want your dog to perform more than one astonishingly brilliant trick in a row to earn said reward. BUT! You want your wonderful and special dog to realize that, while a treat is not in the picture right now, you know he did that trick perfectly, and you want him to know that you know it, and that a reward is definitely in his near future.

Similarly, you need to be able to let Rover know when he's barking up the wrong tree, trick-wise. This requires a special signal between you and your dog. It can be anything you want it to be. When I used to work at a wild animal park, they used whistles and pipes and words. Some people use clickers. I recommend the least amount of gear possible. Keep it simple. Try words and tones that work for you. I usually use the word, "goooooood," very drawn out, over and over to let my dog know he's on the right track, then, "yay" or "woo hoo" to let him know he's finished and it was right. I use "nope" or "too bad, so sad" in a very matter of fact tone to let him know he's gotten it wrong, try again. What we're after is sort of a "you're getting warmer, you're getting colder" set of words. Use them to keep your dog on track. Remember, not giving treats is pretty advanced. We're laying groundwork.

THAT'LL DO!

It's important to remember to have a "release" word to let your dog know that he's offstage now, he can relax. I really, really don't recommend the very popular "ok." Most people use it extensively in conversation and it will result in your dog quitting at very inopportune times. I think my favorite is the herding dog term *that'll do*. It means stop working and come with me. It is effective and distinct.

TRAINING SESSIONS

Training sessions should be more like short play sessions. Lots of animation and a loud, HAPPY voice. They should be short and if your dog is struggling, quit quickly after giving your dog something simple to do, even just making eye contact with you. Always set your dog up to be successful; he's your friend, remember? Think of Timmy and Lassie...talk to your dog as if he's Lassie, even better, *treat* him like he's Lassie! You'll be amazed at how different your relationship will become with that one little change.

You should practice the tricks several times a day and in lots of different places. Practice in the middle of your walk, in the bathroom, in the mall, at Home Depot, and at the park. Practice at your friend's house and in front of the grocery store. I hear it all the time, "he does fine at home, in the kitchen." That's because you've taught him that's the only place it's a trick! He needs to do it everywhere. Remember to have plenty of treats with you in the beginning in case your dog does something genius!

RUDENESS

Your dog should not jump on you or paw you or try to bully you or "mug" you for a treat. If he does, say, "sorry" or "nope" and fold your arms and look away. He may try

harder; stay strong. Don't really look at him and definitely don't push him away with your hands; if you do, he has won a battle. He has made you pay attention to him. You want to present the appearance that there is no way he's getting a treat from you. He should come to his senses quickly and may sit sweetly in front of you, at which time you magically come back to life and praise him like mad! Start working again as if you had never been interrupted. When he tries to mug you again (and he will), or is just being rude, just put the treats away. Let him know that he only gets to work when he's polite. He wants to work! He really does. It gives him a way to get treats. He will learn to be polite very quickly.

THE YO-YO GAME

Actually, in my experience, The Yo-Yo Game is the answer to Loose Leash Walking. When your puppy perfects the game with you standing still, start walking. Hold the treats at about elbow level, close to your abdomen, in a very relaxed way. Take a step, toss a treat to your left, and keep walking. Call the puppy as he's picking up the treat and when he catches up with you, toss another treat. Repeat until the puppy is glued to your side and the only reason he'll leave is if your "push" him away by tossing a treat. He should be trotting next to you, staring up into your face with adoration! What a COOL human! Why would he want to look anywhere else?

This is why I call it the Yo-Yo Game, you "push" him away and he comes back on his own, over and over again! The more you "push" by tossing treats farther and farther away, the more he'll pay attention to you! Start with a treat every step he walks with you, then have him walk 3 steps with you, then 6 and so on. These are going to have to be pretty good treats, because you're not going to use them much. When he's really good in the house, take him outside and do it on-leash on your walks. Start with very frequent treats again, gradually having him work harder and longer for a treat. It WORKS.

The Yo-Yo Game is also great to teach your puppy to come when called, even outside! It's important to give "extended praise" occasionally, extended praise is 17 seconds of praise and tiny treats. The treats should be about the size of a pea, and as you babble nice things to your puppy for 17 seconds, you dole out 17 treats, one per second, as you praise. Puppies should get extended praise at least one time in a training session.

Extended praise is not just for the Yo-Yo Game, but for everything you want the puppy to get better at.

SIT

Sit is a building block for lots of tricks. It's also a great way to control your dog in stressful or distracting situations.

You should even use this method to teach dogs who already know *sit* because of the value of having them learn to watch your hand "lure" them into position.

Start with a handful of driving lesson treats. Hold one in your right hand, between the tips of your thumb and first two fingers. Make sure you have a good grip on it. If your dog is grabby, it's ok to hold it so that your dog can barely touch it, because it's so hidden. Put the tips of your fingers to the tip of his nose; make sure he knows you have something fabulous in there. Slowly, making sure his nose is firmly attached to your fingers, push your fingers forward, into his "space" and back, barely over the top of his head, aiming for the area above his shoulders, behind his head. His nose should follow and throw his balance off a little which should make his butt pop to the floor. Immediately, give the treat and say something profound like, "yay!!!!!" If, during the hand movement, he looks confused, he is, so encourage the process with a reassuring, drawn out,

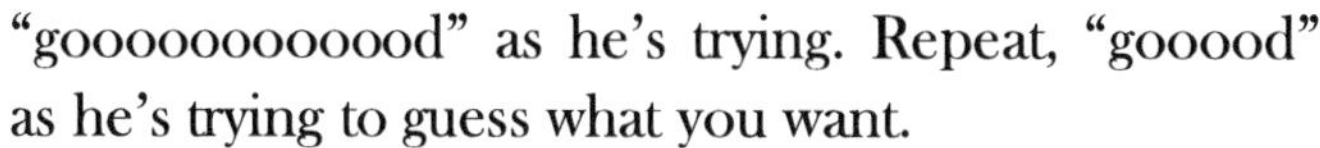

"gooooooooooood" as he's trying. Repeat, "gooood" as he's trying to guess what you want.

Notice that I haven't included saying sit in the instructions. When you use the name of the trick in the beginning, it gets louder and louder and more and more insistent. It will take the place of "gooooooooooood" and you will lose the whole "you're getting warmer" effect. It can cause you to become frustrated and that will make your dog nervous. Dogs don't need words; we will add the name of the trick later. Never forget that your dog has nothing to do all day but study your face and your body posture. That's what dogs do. He will know that you're frustrated before you do! So remember, it's a trick; it's FUN.

As your dog becomes proficient at this fabulous and fun trick and as he starts to do it without you even asking, start to say *sit* just before you give the signal. Then start leaving the treat out of your right hand and giving it with your left. The right hand will still go through the motion, which has now become a hand signal! Soon the hand signal should become smaller and smaller until it's barely noticeable to anybody but you and your dog. COOL TRICK!

Now comes the hard part. To most dogs, *sit* means to sit facing you, close enough to collect his treat. Now you have to teach him that *sit* means sit where he is, facing whatever direction he is facing when he hears the word. This is easiest to do with your dog very close in to you. Your dog will be very confused because you are changing the meaning of the word so be gentle and slow and LURE your dog's head around with the driving lesson treats. Use the treats to move the dog next to you and behind you and ahead of you with his back to you. Practice *sit* and really work on random rewards. Remember to work this trick in lots of different places.

DOWN

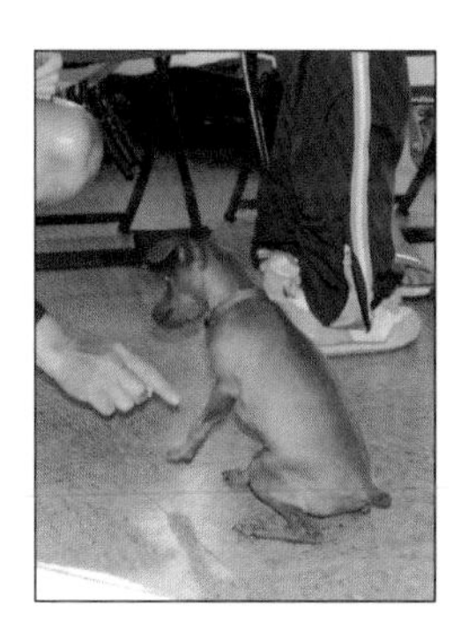

Down is a natural next step from *sit.* Have a lot of treats in your left hand and your one luring treat in your right. With your dog in the *sit* position, get his nose firmly attached to your hand and slowly move your treat down to the toenails of his front feet. Some dogs will respond best if you then push the treat, slowly, under their belly and some dogs do best if you drag it slowly forward, away from their paws. You will know when you try it with your dog. In all cases, the instant (!) your dog's butt comes up off the ground, say your, "nope" word and pull the treat away from him and back to your chest. Start all over from *sit.* You will be surprised at how quickly he figures out that what you're trying to teach him has SOMETHING to do with keeping his butt on the ground. You'll see him trying; it's really cute. Keep giving him his "you're getting warmer" words, keep encouraging. When both elbows are on the ground, say, "yay"! Give him a treat (or a bunch) from your left hand. You may have to ask your dog to *sit* many times to get him to *down.* Remember that *sit* is still a trick and you need to reward it from time to time. Don't take it for granted.

Work this trick all over the place too. Then do it from all the different positions you're doing *sit* from. Then, do *down* without starting from *sit.* It's really hard! But you can do it. As he starts being reliable, start adding the word "down" just before you give the hand signal. Soon he'll start it as soon as he hears the word.

Roll over

This one has great "wow" value! People will be very impressed and it boosts your dog's confidence when he has to roll over in public. It teaches him that he can trust you, even when he's in a really vulnerable position.

Start with your dog in the *down*. Hopefully, he'll already be resting on one hip rather than completely straight up. If not, sweep a treat (in your right hand) from in front of him around toward his hip. Most dogs will roll onto the opposite hip to get the treat. He might jump up. If he does, immediately give your "you're getting colder" word and zip the treat away, back up to your chest, then try again. Try each hip to see which one works best for him. Dogs are "sided" like humans are "handed" as far as left and right. You'll notice a definite difference in which one is easier for him.

Once your dog picks a hip, make sure his nose is firmly attached to your fingers (this definitely calls for a driving lesson treat). Sloooooowly sweep a handful of treats in your right hand from in front of him, low to the ground, back, just past his elbow on the side his legs are pointing to. SLOW is the key. Start to move the treat up from his elbow to his shoulder. Make sure he's with you. His head is twisted around and he's trying to get the treat from the middle of his back. This should force him over onto his side, with his head still reaching toward his back. At this point, with some dogs, you will need to let them get the treat, but keep your hand moving, almost so they don't realize they're tipping over 'til they've tipped. Continue to move your hand across his back and his head follows your hand and his body follows his head and before either of you know it, he's rolled over! Have a party! Whoop it up! Lots of treats, then try again.

As your dog starts getting it, start giving the treat with your left (non-luring) hand. Make your hand signal smaller and smaller and start to say *roll over* just at the beginning of the trick. Practice this on soft surfaces at first, then practice this everywhere, like the other tricks. Have other people tell your dog to *roll over.* The more people he'll do it for, the better.

TOUCH

Touch is really fun and easy. Much easier than roll over! Use this one to give your dog a break from hard stuff.

Start with your dog standing in front of you. Put a treat between your right thumb and forefinger, sort-of in the web. Point your index finger by curling your other fingers into your palm. Show your dog that you have a treat there. When he touches your finger, say, "yay" or whatever word you're using for "you got it right!" and quickly give a treat from your LEFT hand (which has been out of the way). Show your dog the pointed finger again and when he touches it to get the treat, say, "YAY" and give a treat. It usually takes between three and ten repetitions before you see your dog "get it." He will touch your right hand and immediately look at your left hand for a treat.

Start moving your hand around to make your dog touch it on the floor, in the air, on your knee, anywhere. Start rewarding only touches to the tip of your finger. Your dog will try like mad to figure out where the sweet spot is. You can transfer this to a target for agility practice or movie and commercial work! You can use this to teach your dog to flip a light switch or to touch different family members (becomes "find" Dad).

SPIN LEFT AND RIGHT

The hardest part of this trick is deciding whether you mean your left or his left! Think of words to use for this trick, which teaches your dog to spin either left or right, on cue. I've heard people use "which way does the clock go?" or "where's your tail?" for clockwise and "turn back time" or "double check" for counter clockwise. I've also heard "wipe your feet" and "better" for each direction. So be creative and use words that will be easy for you to remember which cue fits which direction.

You need to have forward motion from your dog to have this be easy, so start with your dog in front of you, just standing. Hold your treat in your right hand, lure him toward you, and then as he gets close to your legs, lure his whole body into a circle in front of you. You're basically trying to get him to chase his tail, but he's chasing the treat instead. When he's completed the circle, give a treat with your left hand. Remember to encourage him with your "you're getting warmer" word and celebrate his success with a "yay." This trick can be used later to help him learn to "flip" into a gorgeous heel position. Some dogs may get stuck in *sit.* This is when you need to make sure you're getting forward motion. Remember the lure forward to get him out of *sit.*

Stick 'em up! (or beg)

This is my take on *beg* which is a really cute trick but I like to change things around. I encourage you to use any words or cues that make you happy and make your tricks more exciting or cute.

With your dog sitting in front of you, facing you, point your finger as you did for *touch*. Get your dog's nose firmly attached to your finger by letting him smell a delicious treat. Slowly start to push your hand up and over his head as you did when you were teaching *sit* but raise your hand a tiny bit higher, encouraging him up onto his haunches.

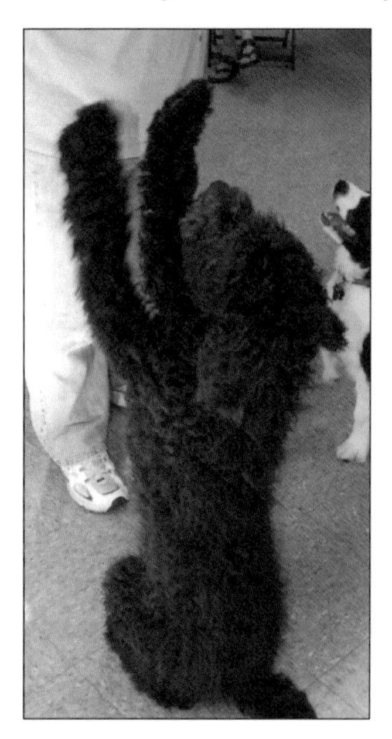

If he jumps for your hand, try it again and keep your hand lower. If his butt comes up, the treat goes away. It's really important for his bottom to stay on the floor, otherwise the trick becomes "stand on your hind legs" which can be cute, but it's not what we're teaching right now. You almost want to push his front legs up, off the floor by pushing on his nose. Remember to use your encouraging word or your "sorry" or "nope" if his bottom comes up.

Reward the smallest steps when you begin, as most dogs find this position a little scary at first. Gradually start asking for more balance and longer times up on his haunches. Really yell, "YAY" if he throws his feet up to catch his balance, this will give him the idea that you'd like to have his feet up and pretty.

It's important not to let him use his feet on your hand to balance himself. Let him work to keep his balance. Some dogs do better with this if you start them with their back in a corner for better balance.

CRAWL

In order to do *crawl* start from *down.* Hold your hand on the ground, in front of your dog's nose, barely out of his reach. Start to move your hand an inch or two farther away. Your dog may paw at your hand or may stand up. If his butt comes off the ground, the treat goes away. Aim for getting him to inch forward on his belly. If he moves forward an inch, say, "YAY" and give him a treat with your other hand! Then ask for two inches. When he gets it, you will see him actually crawl. As you start to be able to get this with just a hand signal, start adding in a verbal cue...like *crawl.*

BANG! (OR PLAY DEAD)

This trick is a "must have," not just because it's cute, but due to the control you can achieve with it. You can use it at the vet to help keep your dog calm and help with exams. Start as you did for *crawl* but as your dog starts into his crawl, move your hand across him as you would for *roll over* and stop him as he rolls onto his side. Lure his head down so he's flat out. As he starts to master this, add the verbal cue just before your hand signal (moving your hand into the gesture that gets him on his side).

To make this just like in the movies, teach him to stay down no matter what. Touch his legs, his head, his ears. Roll him to his other side. Then, when you are really good at it, pick him up. Teach him to keep his head down. This is sooooo cool!

BE JOHN WAYNE!

Or your favorite action hero. Combine *stick 'em up, crawl,* and *bang* and have your dog put on a show. Start with him sitting up on his rear, with his front feet in the air. Then pretend to shoot him and have him crawl (you could even incorporate spinning into this

routine) 'til he rolls to his side and can go on no longer...you go over to check to see if he's faking it (lift a leg, etc.) then pick him up to take him to the hospital. The release word for this could be something like "Vet" or "Gosh, I'm afraid to see the size of this," "BILL," or...something cute.

As you can see, you can do lots of fun things with tricks. The more you practice in strange places, the better your dog will do. Have fun and PLAY!

HAVE FUN!

Well, you have a long and wonderful journey ahead of you. It will be fun and frustrating and SO rewarding. I'm very excited for you and hope that you "got" that puppy training is very logical, not intuitive. If you feel that your emotions are in play, back up and look at why your puppy is doing what he's doing. How is he getting rewarded? When he jumps on people do they coo and pet him? Teach him to sit and hold a treat in front of his nose while he's sitting, when he's been good for a minute or so, call it quits, give him the treat and repeat until it's old to him. When he gets into the trash does he get food? PUT THE TRASH AWAY. I know, you want a dog that can handle having the trash down; we don't let kids drive 'til they're 16 for a reason. They're too young to handle the responsibility! If he starts acting like a butthead, push your emotions aside. It's nothing personal, he's a dog and no, he's not trying to spite you and no, he doesn't know better. Believe him when he uses his behavior to tell you he can't handle the freedom you've given him and the responsibility he's too young for.

Enjoy your puppy. They're puppies for such a short time. When you find yourself chafing because he's still acting like a puppy, remember that this is a dog you'll have for more that a decade; and the time we put into them now will make that decade much more fun and rewarding for both of you!

There are so many fun activities to do with your puppy/dog. Have fun. You can earn titles in everything from dancing to backpacking. Dogs pull carts and scooters and sleds, they comfort people in rest homes and hospitals. They herd sheep and cattle and do tricks to entertain kids. Dogs are amazing companions. Make sure your dog is well socialized and has the manners necessary to make him a part of your life outside your home.

Enroll in all kinds of classes taught by trainers who encourage you to challenge your dog in a non-violent way. Be your dog's advocate. There are trainers with better public relations firms than dog training skills and those are the ones who always seem to end up on television. They can do a lot of damage in a very short time. Running a don't-try-this-at-home warning across the screen is a good bet that the methods are foolish! Don't let any trainer cause you to hurt your dog or damage your relationship.

Enjoy your dog!

ABOUT THE AUTHOR

Trish Wamsat is a native Californian who grew up in the San Francisco Bay area. She was born an animal lover. She took horseback riding lessons, walked neighbors' dogs, and, as a 9 year old, received a cockapoo puppy named Princess. In later years, she was asked to present her pet snakes, crickets, and rats in various elementary school class rooms to teach the other kids about them.

Trish has an extraordinary love of books (animal books) and quickly exhausted her school libraries' supplies of horse and dog stories. In high school, she joined Future Farmers of America and raised rabbits, cattle and sheep, learning animal husbandry and public speaking. It was then that Trish took her first dog trainer's course and was hired by the company as a regional manager upon graduating the course.

While still in high school, she got a job at a wildlife/marine park where she learned more about animals and training. During the "off" season, she was soon hired as an assistant at a police dog training kennel, where ground-breaking training was taking place with Beagles learning to detect termites.

Since then, Trish has spent much of the past 30 years conducting dog training classes and providing private consultations. She has worked as a veterinary technician and is currently employed by Adobe Animal Hospital in Los Altos, California, where she continues to refine and redefine her training skills. Trish participates in frequent continuing education with various trainers and behaviorists and is consulted in most of the behavior cases handled by the 23 full time vets at Adobe.

Trish has spent a lot of time fostering rescued dogs and placing them in great homes. Her family, including her son, Ashton, and niece, Grace (pictured above with the author) support Trish in all of her endeavors!

Printed in the United States
113280LV00001B

9780977109166